Transforming Primary Mathematics

'Lively and thought provoking at a key time in the development of primary mathematics teaching and learning. It offers a very much richer model of mathematics learning than is available to many young learners and has the potential to have a real impact on the way mathematics is taught.'

Jan Winter, *Senior Lecturer in Education, University of Bristol, UK*

- What is good mathematics teaching?
- What is mathematics teaching good for?
- Who is mathematics teaching for?

These are just some of the questions addressed in *Transforming Primary Mathematics*, a highly timely new resource for teachers which accessibly sets out the key theories and latest research in primary maths today.

Underpinned by findings from the largest research programme into primary mathematics funded in recent years, *Transforming Primary Mathematics* offers a clear, practical approach to implementing fundamental change in curriculum, classroom environment and teaching styles.

Written by one of the top experts in mathematics education, it offers an inspiring, sometimes controversial, and often unconventional look at the subject of mathematics, by:

- endorsing the use of a 'new mathematics' – one based on problem solving, modelling and inquiry, not on abstract rules, memorizing, and regurgitation
- arguing that there is more to maths teaching than 'death by a thousand worksheets'
- challenging norms, such as the practice of sorting children into sets based on their perceived mathematical ability
- asking whether this mathematical ability is innate or a result of social practices
- upholding the idea that mathematics teaching is an *adaptive* challenge, rather than a *technical* problem
- advocating an environment where teachers are encouraged to take risks
- looking at how best to prepare learners for an unknown future
- encouraging reflection on teachers' own beliefs and values about mathematics.

Transforming Primary Mathematics is for all primary school teachers who want to make mathematics welcoming, engaging, inclusive and successful.

Mike Askew is Professor of Primary Education at Monash University, Melbourne, Australia. Until recently he was Professor of Mathematics Education at King's College, University of London, UK. A former primary school teacher, he now researches, speaks and writes on teaching and learning primary mathematics.

Transforming Primary Mathematics

Mike Askew

Routledge
Taylor & Francis Group

LONDON AND NEW YORK

First published 2012
by Routledge
2 Park Square, Milton Park, Abingdon, Oxon OX14 4RN

Simultaneously published in the USA and Canada
by Routledge
711 Third Avenue, New York, NY 10017

Routledge is an imprint of the Taylor & Francis Group, an informa business

British Library Cataloguing in Publication Data
A catalogue record for this book is available from the British Library

Library of Congress Cataloging-in-Publication Data
Askew, Mike.
   Transforming primary mathematics/Mike Askew.
       p. cm.
   1. Mathematics – Study and teaching (Elementary)   I. Title.
   QA135.6.A85 2011
   372.72 – dc22   2011004650

ISBN: 978–0-415–60701–8 (hbk)
ISBN: 978–0-415–60702–5 (pbk)
ISBN: 978–0-203–80674–6 (ebk)

Typeset in Galliard
by Florence Production Ltd, Stoodleigh, Devon

Printed and bound in Great Britain by
TJ International Ltd, Padstow, Cornwall

Dedication

For Doreen, with love and thanks for teaching me to jive.

Contents

Figures

Preface

'Look behind you.' As a child a highlight of each year was our family trip to the pantomime. I loved the theatre and got to know the various pantomime plots off by heart. Every pantomime revolves around the big 'transformation' scene. Cinderella's humble pumpkin is transformed into a glittering coach, Aladdin's shabby laundry into a splendid palace, and Jack's few beans into a giant beanstalk. With drum rolls and flashing lights, these scenes realize the magic of the theatre. But as well as the spectacle of worldly trans-formation, these moments mark a turning point, a transformation, for the lead characters. Cinderella shall go to the ball, Aladdin can woo a princess, and Jack gets to kill giants. They are not the people they were before.

'Transforming primary mathematics' I hope invokes these two senses of transformation. Mathematics can perform magic on the world; letting us see patterns and regularity where previously we might only have noticed chaos and confusion. And, if we let it, the magic of mathematics can transform us too.

Some background

Like our pantomime hero setting out on a journey, this book, in part, is a personal journey. Let me set the context by telling something of my own story. I enjoyed maths at school and was 'good' at it, although I realize now that that largely meant I was able to remember rules. It seemed inevitable that I should do a maths degree, so I did, but half-way through realized I actually understood rather little of what was going on in class. Like many others, I fell out of love with maths. Leaving university I had no career in mind but landed a year working at the Open University on a history of mathematics project. Two things happened that year that shaped everything I've done since. First, I got involved in an after-school project working with seven- to eleven-year-olds. I was – still am – struck by the energy and enthusiasm for learning that children of this age display and, although becoming a teacher had not been something I had thought I might want to do, I applied for and was accepted onto the primary teacher education course at Goldsmiths' College in London. The second thing was that in the summer before I went to Goldsmiths' the Open University gave me the chance to teach at their Mathematics Foundation course summer school. There, John Mason introduced me to a new mathematics – one based on problem solving, modeling and inquiry, not on abstract rules, memorizing, and regurgitation. Thanks to John, I began to fall back in love with mathematics.

I taught in primary schools for several years before getting a job in initial teacher education, first at what is now the University of Kingston (then only a polytechnic) and then the University of Greenwich (at that time Avery Hill College), eventually taking up post at King's College, London. Until the move to King's my work was in initial teacher education: once at King's the focus shifted to research. From my first research project looking at problem solving in the (then new and controversial) National Curriculum, a series of projects culminated in a highlight of my time at King's: the five-year longitudinal Leverhulme research program, directed by Margaret Brown. Over the five years of that program it was a pleasure and a privilege to visit numerous mathematics lessons from Reception to Year 6. As a researcher I learnt a huge amount. And yet.

And yet, I was uneasy. The lessons that I saw were fine, good even. The thing was that they were not that much different from what I could remember lessons being like when I had been at primary school. Behind the obvious changes like desks being replaced by tables and chalking giving way to felt tips, most of the lessons followed a structure that echoed how I had been taught: the teacher 'modeling' what to do on the board and the children going off to, individually, complete tasks, most often in the form of worksheets. My unease arose from how little I saw of what had been recommended in the research that I had been reading over the years. Problem solving was not a central focus to lessons, as many writers had advocated. Children sat in groups but did not really work together, despite what I'd read about the power of group work. Talk was mostly limited to answering closed questions, not the lively discussion of mathematical ideas that research advocated.

I began to wonder if the stereotype of academics in ivory towers was accurate. When teachers said that researchers were out of touch with the reality of classrooms, or told me in professional development sessions that 'my kids would not be able to do that', perhaps they were right. Perhaps the reality of teaching mathematics is that it is, if not actually dull, not as engaging and varied as I'd come to believe it could be.

Although not as dramatic as waking up and finding a giant beanstalk in the back garden, this was a transformative moment for me. I decided the only way to test out what I'd come to believe about teaching primary maths was to get back to teaching it. I didn't go back full time into the classroom (selfishly I was only interested in the mathematics) but sought out opportunities to work more closely alongside teachers, trying things out and seeing how children responded.

My first steps on this journey were to go part-time at King's to be able to spend more time in schools. I was pleased to spend a lot of time at Old Ford Primary in the East End of London where the staff there indulged me in trying out many of the ideas that I had been reading about. Many other teachers in and around London also invited me into their classrooms to work alongside them and this further convinced me that there could be more to maths teaching than 'death by a thousand worksheets'.

I also arranged to visit Cathy Fosnot's 'Maths in the City' project in New York. This was a project that had been developed with researchers from the Freudenthal Institute in the Netherlands and the work there on 'realistic' mathematics education. A central tenet of the work in NY and in the Netherlands was to put problem solving at the forefront of mathematics lessons, to build mathematical understandings out of solving problems. I was keen to see what this looked like in action.

The work of Cathy and her team was exciting and inspiring and I couldn't believe my luck when Cathy asked if I would like to go there to work on the project for a year. I did and taught alongside teachers in many schools across Manhattan and Brooklyn. This gave me a sense of the possible and renewed my energy – the mathematics lessons that I saw there did engage the children in meaningful dialogue around big ideas in mathematics, did involve them in problem solving, did embody the ideals that I had read about.

And so I came to believe that primary mathematics can be different, can be based around problem solving, can be transformative. The stories here are stories of the possible. I am not saying that all mathematics teaching should be the way I present it here, but I do suggest that the approaches that I advocate can make teaching and learning maths more satisfying for everyone.

Chapter 1

Introduction

Some people I've encountered in various phases of my career seem more certain about everything than I am about anything. That kind of certainty . . . [displays] an attitude that seems to misunderstand the very nature of reality – its complexity and ambiguity – and thereby to provide a rather poor basis for working through decisions in a way that is likely to lead to better results.

(Rubin and Weisberg 2003)

Is there a 'problem' in primary mathematics education?

The wealth of books and resources available supporting the teaching of primary mathematics suggests there must be a problem with how it is currently taught and learnt, otherwise there would not be a big market for these products. And the media keeps suggesting that too many children leave English primary schools without sufficient mathematics. However, the majority of mathematics lessons that I have been privileged to visit are not unpleasant experiences. Teachers are supportive and children are engaged in mathematics that seems purposeful. If the children do not find maths terribly exciting, at least they do not appear to be stressed. No, I do not think there is a big problem in primary mathematics.

Yet I still believe and hope that learning mathematics in primary schools could be an exciting (in a calm sort of way) experience for more children and open up the possibility of mathematics being something that they *want* to pursue beyond what they are *required* to do. The research evidence, and my experiences, lead me to believe that making mathematics more engaging and at the same time more challenging will lead to higher standards. Contrary to popular opinion, most children rise to the challenge of 'hard' mathematics rather than shy away from it. Children accepting challenging mathematics is, however, dependent upon a number of factors including: a particular style of classroom ethos; close attention to the mathematical challenges presented; support for children in their efforts. The purpose of this book is to explore each of these.

This introductory argument revolves around three questions.

- *What* is good mathematics teaching?
- What is mathematics teaching *good for*?
- *Who* is mathematics teaching for?

What is good mathematics teaching?

This is what the majority of books and articles and research papers set out to address. In writing this book I am adding to the mountain of advice (although, as I hope will become clear, I offer my advice as conditional – it might work – rather than dogmatic shoulds). I started teaching in the late 1970s and moved into research in the early 1990s: most of my career has been directed toward trying to answer this question. I don't think I'll ever have the definitive answer to it. That is because the nature of teaching is, and always will be, an *adaptive* challenge, rather than a *technical* problem (Heifetz, Linsky *et al.* 2009).

Heifetz *et al.* argue that we can find solutions to technical problems through our current expertise. Plenty surround us in our daily lives. Recently I had to travel from Sheffield to London and I needed to be in London by a certain time. The Internet provided me with the tools to plan my journey, book my train ticket, and pay online so I could travel relaxed in the knowledge that none of these decisions or actions had to be done at the last minute. Next time I have a similar 'technical problem' I'll be familiar with the steps to go through to solve it.

In contrast, adaptive challenges require solutions that have yet to be found; solutions that are different from current practices. Teaching mathematics for the uncertain times we live in is an adaptive challenge. It is imaginable that future generations will meet this adaptive challenge by deciding to stop teaching mathematics altogether. I cannot imagine why or how that could come about, but my lack of imagination is no reason for assuming that maths education needs to continue in its current form. No doubt there must have been moments in time when schoolmasters could not imagine any education could be complete without a sound grounding in Latin or Greek, but where are they now?

Policy initiatives in England, and elsewhere, tend to treat the teaching and learning of mathematics in primary schools as a technical problem: we already know from current practices the solution to engaging children and raising standards. If teachers can be better 'trained' to 'deliver' mathematics using existing techniques then all will be well. While teaching arithmetic to Victorian clerks might have been a technical problem, teaching mathematics now is too complex to be reducible to a prescriptive set of techniques. We need to work with a view of mathematics teaching as an adaptive challenge. That means trying out new ways to teach and in particular allowing pedagogies to emerge rather than imposing them.

This does not negate the fact that, literally, tomorrow children across the globe are going to go into mathematics lessons. We cannot use pedagogies that have not yet been invented to teach them – we can only work with what we have got. We have to work with our current knowledge, but that we need to treat that knowledge as 'conditional'. It works to the best of our current knowledge within the current conditions of teaching. But we must be cautious of claims for descriptions of current 'good mathematics teaching' being what is needed in the near, or far, future.

Treating teaching as an adaptive challenge does not, however, suggest an 'anything goes' approach or that teachers simply have to make it up as they go along. We have to work with the best of our current knowledge without that getting set in stone. As teachers we need to be prepared to take some manageable risks. I am sharing in this book what I consider to be some of the 'best' of the current knowledge (that I am aware of) from the research and some stories of the manageable risks that, working together, teachers and I have tried.

Stop teaching mathematics

Surprising as it may seem, one school district in the USA (Manchester, New Hampshire) did experiment with taking mathematics out of the primary (elementary) curriculum. Teachers' concerns over the burdens of a too heavy curriculum led the district education officers to persuade half of the schools to drop formal mathematics lessons from the timetable. They did not remove mathematics completely from the curriculum: the teachers were encouraged to pick up and teach mathematical ideas as they arose in other subjects. So, for example, measuring could be taught in the context of science lessons; averages and percentages in the context of a topic such as looking at sport and its statistics. There was a state test toward the end of the final year of elementary school (when children were around eleven years old), so the officers agreed that teachers could reinstate mathematics lessons in that final year to ensure the children were familiar with the content and conventions of the test. To check out the impact of the initiative, they also gave all the children a separate test of mathematical problem solving.

When the results of the state test came in, it was not possible to distinguish the children who had been in the mathematics-lessons-free classrooms from those who had been taught it formally throughout their elementary school years. Perhaps more strikingly, on the problem-solving assessment the children who had been taught in the mathematics-in-context schools significantly out-performed the others (Benezet 1935a, b, c).

All this took place in the 1930s; in these days of high-stakes tests and accountability, I doubt anyone anywhere would be brave enough to replicate this experiment.

What is mathematics teaching good for?

At first sight the answer to this may seem glaringly obvious and circular. Whatever can mathematics teaching be good for other than teaching mathematics? A bit like asking 'what is a sieve good for?', or 'what is in this can of beans?' The answer is in the question.

Any teaching, including the particular case of mathematics, actually teaches far more than the 'content': children are learning much more than just mathematics in mathematics lessons. They are learning a lot about themselves and about their peers and about relationships. A second aim of this book is to look at some of the other things that get learned alongside mathematics and to argue for giving these equal, if not more, importance as the content. These are not 'either/or' aims of mathematics teaching, but complementary. What children learn about themselves and others directly impacts on the learning of mathematics at the same time as their experiences in mathematics lessons influence this other learning.

Who is mathematics teaching for?

Again we can take the obvious answer of the children in the class. Cynics may say that in the current climate of national testing then mathematics teaching is for those who compile the league tables – the children are only a means to the end of making sure schools meet targets.

I want to add that today's teaching is, in part, for the adult that the child will become. Given the rate of change that we are going through – generally accepted by commentators, as the most rapid ever in our history – how best to prepare learners for an unknown future is a major challenge. If, as the writer L.P. Hartley said, the past is a foreign country then the future is an alien one. They not only do things differently there, they do different things. This makes the challenge for the primary mathematics teacher of today increasingly difficult. We cannot predict the future, and yet we need to prepare children for this uncertainty.

There is much talk of 'equipping' pupils for the future that they will be 'entering' when they leave school. But the future is not a place that exists, simply waiting for pupils to enter it. The pupils of today are the creators of future societies, not visitors to them. Does mathematics education have a role to play in helping prepare children for creating their futures? I think it does.

For example, current practices establish norms about different abilities in mathematics and enact these through practices such as sorting pupils into high, medium and low groups and labeling individuals – level 4, gifted and talented, and so forth. Society at large also labels people, for example in terms of their 'race'. Genetics studies now demonstrate that there is no biological basis to the notion of race, that this is a construct that is socially created through interaction and relationships and social practices; there is no reality to the idea of race outside the social. Research now also challenges the long-held view that mathematical ability is innate and fixed (Shenk 2010). If the reality of mathematical ability is ungrounded and differences in attainment largely come about from social practices, then we need to look at the impact of these on learning mathematics and to question them. But looking beyond the classroom the practice of grouping and labeling children in mathematics legitimizes grouping and labeling more broadly and so may contribute to sustaining societal issues such as race. We have to accept that there may be a relationship between divided mathematics classes and divided communities.

Given the impossibility of predicting the future the solution is not to look back and return to 'the basics' as some would advocate. Nor can we justify dull mathematics teaching on the 'trust me, you'll need this later' argument. Learning and teaching have to be worthwhile experiences in the here and now, while keeping an eye on the future horizon. Looking forward while attending to the present is a big challenge to today's mathematics classrooms.

The joy of mathematics

Imagine two semi-circles, one much bigger than the other and joined at one end of each of their diagonals (Figure 1.1).

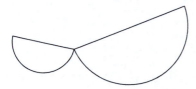

Figure 1.1 Two semi-circles joined at a point

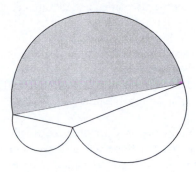

Figure 1.2 A large third semi-circle joining the original two

Suppose they are connected by a third semi-circle meeting them at the open ends of their diameters. If the angle between the two original semi-circles is large enough, then it is clear by looking (by inspection as mathematicians like to call it – not to be confused with school inspection) that the area of the third, new, semi-circle must be much greater than the area of the two original semi-circles put together (Figure 1.2).

On the other hand, if the angle between the two semi-circles is small, then it is immediately obvious that the area of the new semi-circle is much smaller (you can actually see this I hope from Figure 1.3). In general one should always be wary when a mathematician says something is 'obvious'. There is a story, apocryphal but with a grain of truth, of a mathematician giving a lecture and in the middle of developing an argument saying 'it obviously follows that . . . at least I think it follows . . .' and, with a furrowed brow, walked out of the lecture hall. Returning 20 minutes later he continued the lecture with 'yes, it is obvious that'!

OK, now you have to use some imagination to bring these two diagrams to life. Imagine that the point at which the two triangles are joined is a hinge of sorts and they can move closer together or further apart. The size of the third semi-circle is, unlike the other two, not fixed and changes accordingly as the original two semi-circles move together or apart. Got the moving picture? So, as illustrated in Figure 1.2 at one extreme the area of the third, dependent, semi-circle is greater than the sum of the areas of the other two and, at the other extreme (Figure 1.3), it is smaller than their sum. In the movement of the two semi-circles from one extreme to the other, there has to be a point at which the area

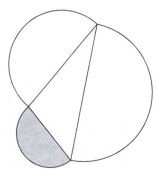

Figure 1.3 A small third semi-circle joining the original two

of the third semi-circle is precisely equal to the sum of the other two areas added together. Other than at this singular point of balance there is not much that can be said about the relationship between the areas of the three semi-circles. But in that sea of uncertainty there is this one place of calm, of balance. And it happens that this position of calm occurs when the angle between the two semi-circles is exactly 90 degrees.

If this is beginning to sound familiar then you will have spotted that the first person credited with finding this oasis of calm was Pythagoras, although his jolly old theorem is presented as squares rather than semi-circles.

What is the point of this diversion? Well, first of all, Pythagoras' theorem is usually taught and learnt as a piece of inert abstract knowledge. What I hope this little thought experiment demonstrates is the power of the mathematician's desire to find and bring order to a world of variation and uncertainty. As Bruner (1979) described it, the move from the complex to the predictable and simple is 'the most fundamental form of pleasure in man's intellectual life' (p. 110). Setting aside the masculinity of the quote (although some might argue that pleasure from simplicity is a predominantly male perspective) when mathematicians strive towards predictability and simplicity, in the setting up of mathematical models of the world, they do not remove the unpredictability and complexity of the world. Pythagoras' theorem marks a moment of balance, and locating this within the complex world of uncertain relationships of areas (as I have tried to do in the above description) makes both – the real world with its complexity *and* the mathematical world with its simplicity – more wondrous. Pythagoras' theorem is a mathematical haiku, capturing a moment of calm and reflection leading to insight.

To take an example closer to primary mathematics look at just some of the infinite range of real-world situations that can be modeled by the single mathematical expression 3×4:

- A tray of muffins, four rows by three;
- Four bags, each containing three apples;
- If I have three t-shirts and four pairs of shorts, the number of days that I can go out in t-shirt and shorts and not wear the same combination twice;
- The number of sprats a mother shark eats if she eats four for every one her baby eats and the baby eats three;
- The length of a rope that is needed to make four skipping ropes each of which are 3 meters long;
- The weight of a bag of cement that is four times as heavy as a 3 kg bag;
- And so on.

The power of mathematics lies in this compactness of representation but all too often the singularity of the mathematics is matched with a singular 'real' experience of it. In the case of multiplication this is usually repeated addition. Why is this? First I think because of the assumption that the real-world model of repeated addition is only there to help children actually calculate the answer to 3×4. That, however unarticulated (or shouted out loud in some quarters), arithmetical competency (as measured by being able to correctly calculate with increasingly awkward numbers) is still thought of as the overarching goal of primary mathematics. I do not agree: we have cheap, convenient and accessible technology now that can do such calculations more accurately. Calculators and computers were not available to the Victorians, the originators of the 'gold standard' of arithmetic, but had they been I bet Bob Cratchit would have pounced on them. Second, the belief that children get confused by too many ideas (this is still linked to the first point – the ideas confuse because they get in the way of being able to 'do' the calculation). I don't think children are confused by too many ideas – most thrive on them. But importantly this limited set of ways of thinking about something even as 'simple' as 3 × 4 diminishes the possibility of them having a sense of the power of mathematics and of them coming to care for mathematics.

Mindfulness and variation

These are two themes that run through this book that I examine in greater detail in the coming chapters but I use this example from Pythagoras to provide a brief 'advance organizer' (Ausubel 1968) of them.

Mindfulness comes from the work of Ellen Langer, a psychologist whose body of work has demonstrated many times over how presenting knowledge as done-and-dusted facts limits people's learning. Pythagoras' theorem is usually presented in that way. Even when presented in a fashion that invites learners to explore the relationship between the areas of the squares, the fact that this works for a right-angled triangle is usually taken as a given: the learner is not invited to explore the relationship in non-right-angled triangles. In setting up the idea in the dynamic way that I described I am trying to introduce what Langer identifies as a key element, the element of *conditionality* (Langer 1997). It *could* be that the third area is greater than the other two; it *could* be that it is less and it *could* even be that it is the same. This latter state then becomes the interesting one to explore, but the awareness of this interest has come about as result of the conditionality of the relationship with the other two states.

This awareness of conditionality is brought about by the *variation* that the learner experiences. In teaching Pythagoras' theorem what is traditionally varied is the size of the triangle: the angle between the two sides opposite the longest side is not varied; where is the interest in that? Well, the interest in that is precisely that changing the angle does make things rather less interesting. But you would not know that until the angle had been varied. What else could be varied? By swapping squares for semi-circles, one may become mindful that the fact that Pythagoras chose to use squares is not that central to his theorem (although calculating the areas of squares is easier than semi-circles). Pythagoras was mindful of the conditions under which everything balances, not concerned to give his name to a theorem that causes grief to many.

Outline for the rest of the book

In Part One I set out the general arguments underpinning why I think we need to change the way that we teach primary mathematics. Chapter 2 looks at some current research and thinking about learning. I argue here that one of the biggest and most influential changes that we could make would be to look at learning as something broader than simply what happens in the minds of individual children. While learning certainly has an individual component to it, difficulties arise when we place too much emphasis on the individual and the purely cognitive. The attention on the individual and internal has the effect of making the actions of individual learners the focus of much mathematics teaching. I argue that we need to look at learning as a whole activity system, of which the individual learner is only one part. Broadening out the focus means attending to the learning that we hope pairs of children will make and also the learning that a whole class might engage in. The central thesis to this argument is that collective learning is more than the sum of the parts, more than the sum of the learning of the individuals in the collective. By also attending to the learning of the collective (and sub-groups, and pairs within the collective) the learning of individuals will progress as a consequence.

Chapter 3 turns our attention to thinking about the curriculum. Just as learning traditionally focuses on parts of the system – individual learners – so too much advice focuses on slicing mathematics up into parts: specific objectives, isolated lessons, fragmented topics. This breaking down of teaching into parts provides the illusion of teaching directly controlling learning. I argue that just as we need to take a broader view of learning, so we need to take a broader view of teaching and accept that, beyond training children in being able to carry out specific mathematical techniques and procedures, the link between teaching and learning is tenuous. Rather than this being a 'problem' to overcome I suggest that living with the reality of this can make teaching more enjoyable and learning more productive.

Living with teaching and learning as loosely coupled means accepting that in the course of lessons learning needs to 'feedback' into teaching – that everyone is learning in a lesson and a certain amount of the direction of lessons cannot be predicted but needs to be picked up and followed as a result of the learning that is emerging in these lessons. Rather than seeing teaching as the following of a lesson script that has a completely predictable set of 'scenes' within it, in Chapter 4 I use the metaphor of improvisational drama to explore how teaching and learning can both emerge from classroom interactions.

If teaching mathematics has an element of improvisation to it, then that is not to suggest that it is all 'made up' as we go along; Part Two looks at this in more detail. Chapter 5 revisits mathematics learning and argues that much of the mathematics children learn needs to be approached 'mindfully' and balanced against developing fluency. In Chapter 6 I draw on a particular theory of how to plan lessons (variation theory) which maximizes the likelihood of children's learning reaching desired outcomes but without assuming that this can be done in ways that totally control the learning.

Chapter 7 shifts our attention to what children could learn within the context of mathematics lessons beyond the content of the mathematics itself: what children might learn about themselves, about learning mathematics and about working with others. In line with the approach taken in the earlier chapters, I do not suggest that these are separate to learning mathematics itself but intimately entwined with it. And that these are important aspects of learning in their own right – possibly even more important than learning mathematics itself.

Chapter 8 develops the themes introduced in Chapter 7 and examines both how and why building supportive classroom mathematical communities is an important part of learning.

Chapter 9 marks the beginning of Part Three, which looks in more detail at putting the ideas from Parts One and Two into practice. I proposed thinking about teaching as requiring attention to three aspects – tasks, tools and talk – the 'teaching tripod'. The nature of classroom tasks is explored in Chapter 9, then Chapters 10 and 11 look at tools and talk respectively. A brief coda rounds off the book.

A word about theory

I have drawn on several theories and have been unashamedly selective in the aspects of these I use to support my argument. Some purists may think I am being theoretically flirtatious (even promiscuous) by inviting so many theorists in. My position is that theory can only go so far in helping us understand the complexity of teaching and learning. Theories are constructed through language. Teaching and learning are constructed through interaction and activity. Any theoretical account of teaching and learning can only ever be a shadow of the 'real thing' and as such will never be able to capture the totality of teaching and learning mathematics. Different theoretical perspectives can, however, provide lenses that might make us 'see' lessons differently and in doing so, make us rethink what we might have come to take for granted. For those of you who do find that the theories I touch on spark an interest, I end each chapter with a couple of suggestions of where more detailed accounts can be found.

Summary

To meet the challenges of mathematics teaching, ways of working in classrooms need to emerge through the joint activity of teachers and children. Learning does not only happen in the minds of individual children – classrooms are learning systems. By attending to how the classroom community grows and learns (teacher and children together) it is possible to create classrooms where children:

*   engage with meaningful mathematics
*   learn that they can learn mathematics
*   develop socially and emotionally
*   realize the importance of inter-dependency.

Part I

Thinking through mathematics

Chapter 2

Thinking about learning

> Learning . . . is more a reaching out than a taking in. It is a participation. It is a process of remembering – in the word's original sense of pulling together the parts of a body into a more complex unity. That is, even though it is often convenient to speak of an agent's knowledge as though it resided within the agent, that knowledge is what defines the agent's relationship to the rest of the world. The agent's activity and identity are inseparable from his, her or its knowledge. Knowing is doing is being.
>
> (Davis, Sumara *et al.* 2000)

In the preface I indicated two aspects of transforming that I want to explore: how mathematics teaching might be transformed and how learners might be transformed through their learning of mathematics. This chapter begins by looking at the former: that mathematics teaching as currently constituted could benefit from being transformed. I want to explore aspects of learning and in particular some commonly held perspectives that need to be complemented with views from a different position as these will inform later discussion of teaching; namely that

- the individual child is at the centre of learning mathematics
- learning mathematics is a process of acquiring knowledge
- acquiring this knowledge is a well-ordered process.

This chapter examines the first of these, while Chapter 3 looks at the latter two. There is of course an element of truth to each of these views. The individual child clearly has a big part to play in learning, say, the recall of multiplication facts or being able to use a ruler accurately. It makes some sense to say that the child who, a little while back, did not know when to use subtraction has now 'got it'. It certainly makes sense to teach adding whole numbers before trying to teach division of fractions. But each of these observations is only part of the story and difficulties arise from acting as though these parts tell the whole story of learning mathematics. For example, if the main focus of our attention is on each individual child then we might treat classes as collections of 30 individuals and in doing so miss much that could be gained by attending to the learning of the whole class, in taking the collective as our 'unit' of learning. In this chapter I look at research and theory that challenges the view of mathematics learning as a solitary activity and explores the possibilities of shifting our attention to collective learning.

Similarly, only focusing on what children are learning in terms of the acquisition of knowledge may distract us from attending to who they are becoming through the processes of this learning: what they are learning, not just about the mathematics, but about themselves and about others. Learning mathematics is not, and cannot be, separated from the project of who young learners are becoming. The comprehensive and recently published Cambridge Primary Review identifies twelve aims for primary education including: 'To promote respect for self, for peers and adults, for other generations, for diversity and difference . . . To understand the essential reciprocity of learning and human relations' (Alexander 2010: 198).

Limiting the focus of mathematics lessons to acquiring knowledge then, at best, may omit opportunities for fostering respect and reciprocity, and, at worst, tacitly condone behaviors that act against these values. There is a moral dimension to mathematics teaching that extends beyond a duty to help children do well in the subject.

Finally, if we treat learning as linear and predictable, then where is the opportunity for creativity? If all lessons have to be built around pre-determined learning outcomes, how can we build on what learners bring to the lesson?

As a counterbalance to these three views I argue that transformative mathematics teaching would pay attention to

- learning as a collective activity
- how learning involves becoming as well as acquiring
- integrating the mathematics that 'emerges' as children work on rich problems and investigations with pre-planned learning intentions.

I am not arguing for replacing the first three views with the second three, that would be as reductionist as only attending to the former. Nor are the three foci of collectivity, becoming and emergence separate. It is the combination of these three together with the more usually accepted views that makes mathematics teaching powerful. I discuss each separately for organizational simplicity rather than theoretical distinction.

There are tensions in resolving the first three perspectives with the second three. Having a vision for how a whole class might be learning and developing must not squeeze out sensitivity to the progress of individuals within that class. Being nice to each other should not get in the way of having conversations about mathematics where someone's ideas might get challenged. Also, teaching is an intentional activity and I am not suggesting that it is sufficient to go into lessons with a vague sense of what mathematics might emerge. On the other hand I am arguing that the model of a totally prescribed (literally pre-written or pre-scripted) lesson that does not allow for contributions from the learners is a limiting experience – for teachers as well as pupils. Tensions, however, are not necessarily a bad thing and cannot, indeed should not, be removed.

Tension gets a bad press in the everyday: we talk of tension headaches, feeling tense, a meeting full of tension. But tension is a necessary part of what makes things work: a suspension bridge without tension won't stay up, muscles work through tension and release. Tensions in teaching cannot be massaged away, but they can be managed. In attending to them, not ignoring them, then mathematics teaching and learning can be more engaging and creative for teachers and learners alike.

The learner at the center

When I was training to be a teacher, we talked a lot about children 'discovering' mathematics. This was the dominant theory of learning mathematics and it meant that as a teacher you needed to provide carefully structured experiences, largely of a practical nature. Children, through their actions on the practical, were expected to discover and then 'abstract' the mathematics that was supposedly embedded in the materials, much as an archeologist might extract (abstract) artifacts buried in the ground through careful digging and sifting. Even as I was teaching and not experienced or brave enough to question this received wisdom it was clear that not all children succeeded in this excavation of mathematics. One famous quote of the time from a boy failing to make the connection between doing calculations and handling blocks summed it up: 'Sums is sums and bricks is bricks' (Hart, Johnson *et al.* 1989). Yet the strong grip of believing priority had to be given to physical experience was enshrined by the Nuffield Primary Mathematics Project, an influential study into the teaching and learning of primary mathematics that had as a central premise the (allegedly) Confucian motto:

I hear and I forget
I see and I remember
I do and I understand.

When it comes to learning mathematics I now think that all three statements are erroneous. Learning can come about just as effectively from hearing or seeing, and doing in the physical sense is no more a guarantee of learning than listening or watching.

The difficulty with the language of discovery is its suggestion that mathematics exists 'out there' in the world, it is 'all around us' and all children have to do is to open their eyes wider, or look more closely, or dig a little deeper, and the mathematics will be revealed. If teaching through discovery learning failed that did not mean that the central premise of the importance of 'doing' needed to be questioned: at best it meant that children had not had enough experience; at worst that they weren't mathematically 'able' to see or discover.

At the time it was popularly held that practices based around discovery learning had emerged out of the theories of Piaget. Thought, Piaget had argued, was a result of internalized activity (actually his argument was both broader and subtler than this but that was the gist used in teacher education) and so activity had to be at the heart of teaching. In fact it now seems that teachers were already using a lot of practical work and Piaget's theories were 'picked up' in order to justify these existing practices (Walkerdine 1984). Whether or not this was the case, the emphasis was firmly on the individual child at the center of learning, a young lone mathematical archeologist on a voyage of discovery.

Through the 1990s views of learning changed, questioning this hierarchy of doing taking precedence over seeing and that in turn over hearing. One idea that then came to be popular was that different learners had different learning styles: one was either an auditory, visual or kinesthetic (doing) learner: VAK. There was no longer a hierarchy to these three modes of experience but each of us had a preference for one over the others. I consider myself to have difficulty visualizing things and I'm not particularly physically adept but I do like playing with words. Clearly I'm an auditory thinker. That's obviously why I began to find mathematics difficult at university: it was the visual thinkers who had the edge on me (although I could not begin to tally up the number of teachers who have told me they find maths difficult because they are visual thinkers).

Time moves on and recent brain research is suggesting that this idea of learning preferences is not a reflection of how the mind actually works. A sense of a preference for one way of learning over the others is a 'real' subjective experience that each of us feels. However, scans of people's brains as they engage in activities show that the regions that deal with the auditory, the visual and the kinesthetic are all active even if the person under the scanner reports only feeling that they are firing on one of these cylinders (Goswami 2007).

The idea of VAK and learning preferences is still quite deeply established in the 'common-sense' knowledge of teaching, even though we now know that learning is multi-sensual and it is important that children have experience of all three modes. I think this account of learning preferences holds its appeal because the center of the learning is still the individual child: the account of the mechanics of learning has simply shifted from the external explorations of the individual learner to their internal preferences. The story has changed, the focus of attention – the individual learner – has not.

Actions and activities

If talk about learning emphasizes the individual, then so does society at large. We live in a culture that reifies the individual. Bookshop shelves of 'self-help' and 'self-development' books are not matched by rows of 'community-help' or 'collective-development' books. Popular reality and talent shows celebrate the individuals who beat off the opposition. We are immersed in a culture that seems to be based on the idea that the community, if it exists at all, is simply the sum of the individuals.

'Western' schools are embedded within this culture of the individual and therefore are not immune to it. I am not part of the culture of 'Eastern' education, but from what I've read about it, the emphasis on the individual is not so dominant in, say, primary schools in Japan, although globalization may be changing their culture. At one level of course learning is an individual achievement: I had to do the necessary practice and chanting to commit my times tables to memory, no-one else could have learnt them for me. But although I was the one who ultimately memorized the tables, that learning was not, could not, be independent of the social and cultural context that I happened to have grown up in. The weekly tables tests at school; the stars for getting them all correct; my parents making sure I practiced; the mood of the teacher in response to test scores – all these, and more, shaped my learning the tables.

I am going to use the label *activity* to describe this total context of coming to learn my tables and distinguish this from the *actions* or behaviors that I personally engaged in. Activity represents the totality of coming to learn anything, and any individual's actions or behaviors are their particular contribution to the activity. I am borrowing this from the work of the Russian theorist Leont'ev who demonstrates the distinction between activity and action from experiences such as going hunting. An individual may be engaged in the activity of hunting for game that will provide the family with food, but only involved in the action of beating the undergrowth to drive game out into the open. The individual's actions do not, on their own, lead directly to the object of the activity – food on the table. In learning my tables, my actions – practicing chanting them, going over them repeatedly – are located and make sense within the broader activity of teacher expectations, parental instruction, relationship with peers: the whole cultural activity that places value on learning the multiplication tables. I was not an isolated player engaged in solitary actions and motivated by some purely internal desire. My learning was inextricable from my network of relationships and joint activity.

Activity goes beyond simply describing what an individual learner is doing, and should not be confused with terms such as 'active learning'. Equally, activity is not meant to suggest learning that involves lots of physical behavior: a mother and child looking quietly at a picture book together are engaged in activity even if the only visible behavior is movement of their eyes.

Activity, as I am using it here, is therefore always a result of particular social, cultural and historical settings. To continue with the example of learning the tables, the social included relationships with parents, teachers and peers, with these not always being aligned with each other. For example, as a learner how does one manage the desire to please the teacher with the potential of subsequent playground teasing for being a 'swot'? Learning your tables is cultural in the sense that it is a valued performance: being born into a nomadic tribe of hunter-gatherers results in growing up in a culture where there would be no value to this performance. And it is historical in that all learning takes place in a particular time: 100 years earlier or later and the situation would be very different. It is also historical in the small-scale sense of the learner's personal history.

Drawing attention to the socio-cultural-historical aspects of learning activity raises (at least) three issues. First, as I have argued, it directs attention to the fact that learning is more than just the behavior of the individual. Second, seeing learning as happening in a stream of 'history' means that it is never 'done' or completed: the child who does not know their tables has not learned them yet, which is different from concluding that they cannot learn them. Third, we need to take the totality of activity into account when planning and carrying out mathematics teaching.

I want to contrast two lessons to illustrate and explore the difference made by thinking about teaching mathematics in terms of activity rather than actions. Both examples are based around introducing six- and seven-year-olds to place value. They took place in the same school, on the same day and the teachers had planned the lessons together, so that each class would have similar experiences.

Place value I

The teacher started off the lesson by explaining the idea of place value through some images on the interactive whiteboard: a series of two-digit numbers were displayed and clicking on each of the digits in the number produced pop-up images of the requisite numbers of tens or units.

The children were then given worksheets that had a list of two-digit numbers: they had to fill in two columns specifying the number of tens and ones in each number. So given, say, 67 they would write 6 in the column headed T and 7 under U, although some children were recording 60 and 7. When they finished that worksheet they went onto a 'harder' one involving HTU.

continued . . .

The teacher had asked me to take the plenary part of the lesson, so I decided to put what the children had been working on into a simple context. I told a story of a friend, Jo, who ran a fruit stall in a market. She sold her fruit in bowls of ten pieces of fruit, rather than by weight. If she had a carton of 67 apples, how many bowls of ten apples would she be able to put out on her stall?

I asked the children to turn and talk to the person they were sitting next to. Despite only minutes before having been recording how many tens there were in a number, it was clear from their talk and accompanying hand actions that nearly all of the class were having to figure out the answer from first principles, counting up or back in tens to see how many bowls of ten apples could be made. Several children appeared to find it difficult to know where to start. Only two quickly made the connection to what they had just been doing. I asked this pair how many bowls Jo would be able to make from a large carton of 236 apples. They were confident that she would be able to make 203 bowls of ten: three from the 30 and another 200 bowls from the other 200 apples.

In my experience this is not an unusual way of teaching place value and the actions of the children during the main part of the lesson can be mapped onto Vygotsky's theories about tool use, a theory developed by, amongst others, Michael Cole (1996). The basic idea is that actions can be examined as the combination of the 'subject' – the individual performing an action – and 'object' – the goal of that action. Many actions directly link the subject and object: Jim wants the vase of flowers on the dining table so he picks them up off the coffee table and moves them. Vygotsky's observation was that most of our subject–object actions are not done directly but are mediated through artifacts or tools. (Chapter 10 develops all this in more detail.) If Jim decides the stems of the roses are too long, rather than snap them off directly, he could use a pair of secateurs to trim them. Physical tools like secateurs extend our 'natural' capacities, and other species have also been shown to use simple tools. What distinguishes human use of tools is that some tools not only enable us to achieve things in our environment that we could not achieve without them, but the tools also have an effect back on us as beings: they are psychological tools (Vygotsky 1986). For Vygotsky, the most powerful psychological tool we have is language. It is a tool that not only enables us to achieve our 'objects' but also fundamentally changes who we are in the process of their use. Jim can try and achieve his object of getting the flowers moved by saying 'Jane, can you put these flowers on the dining-room table please?' and whether Jane moves them or he gets a response along the lines of 'get up and move them yourself' much more is being learned than simply how to get flowers moved. A particular relationship is set up between Jim and Jane that affects them individually and collectively. Learning mathematics has an effect on the individual and relationships just as language does.

To return to the teaching of place value, the 'subject' is the individual learner, and the 'object' is that they should have some understanding of place value. Linking these two cannot be done directly – the learner cannot directly go from not knowing about place value to knowing about it. Teachers provide tools and artifacts that mediate this, through which the learning is assumed to be enabled. In the lesson described, mediating tools and artifacts included the images of tens and ones projected on the whiteboard and worksheets that the children had to complete.

Let me now compare this with a second lesson covering the same topic. I visited the parallel class of children who were about to do the same worksheet on place value. As I was there before the start of the lesson, the teacher and I had time to talk about changing the plan, turning the lesson on its head and starting with the story of my friend Jo.

Place value 2

I began by talking about market stalls and so forth, just as described in the other lesson. Having set it up that Jo puts her fruit into bowls of ten, we asked the children to work in pairs and figure out how many bowls of ten Jo could make from a box of 67 apples. From the experience in the parallel class I did not expect them to quickly know that 67 would allow for six bowls of ten apples. The children were given plain paper and we asked them to work together to figure out the answer. Most of them could do this, but one of the things that became clear was how few of them organized their work in ways that would help them find the answer easily. For example, some children simply drew long lines of apples, until they had drawn 67 and then marked off groups of 10, sometimes getting confused over what would happen at the end of lines.

As they completed the first example, we gave the pairs of children other numbers to work on and when everyone had done two or three 'boxes of fruit', we brought the class together to share some of their work in progress. We looked in particular at the representations of those children who had organized the images into distinct groups of ten. We sent the children off again in their pairs to figure out the numbers of bowls of ten for other totals that we had listed on the board, with everyone now being tuned in to being more organized in their recording.

As the children found the number of bowls that could be made from their boxes of fruit I listed the number of pieces of fruit in the box, the number of bowls and the 'left-overs' in a table on the board. Could the children see any patterns? In pairs the children talked about what they noticed and the class discussed the relationship between the total number of pieces of fruit and the groups of ten and 'left-overs'. This led into a discussion of how our way of recording numbers allows us to easily know the number of groups of ten in a number.

Fruit	Bowls	Left-overs
63	6	3
24	2	4
37	3	7
52	5	2
71	7	1

We can look at this second lesson again in terms of subject–object and mediating tools. A main difference from the other lesson is in the range of mediating tools and artifacts: I include here the 'story' of Jo, the children's own representations and the table of results, as all mediating the children's actions. In what sense is Jo's story a mediating tool? I suggest the context is important here. It is not 'window dressing' to make the task more appealing, nor is it simply an opportunity to apply place value (which most of the children could not do anyway). It is a key mediating tool in helping children find meaning in their actions. First, it provided a context that was already meaningful for the children. They had seen bowls of fruit on sale. But being meaningful here is not simply about relating this to their 'real' lives (isn't school part of your 'real' life?); it is a meaningful context that they can 'mathematize'. This is a key tenet of the work of the Freudenthal Institute building on the work of the mathematics educator Hans Freudenthal.

Freudenthal's approach to learning was that mathematics grew out of the activity of 'mathematising the world' (Freudenthal 1975). Mathematics, as a discipline, did not suddenly spring from nowhere, but is the result of human activity. Place value did not simply 'appear' and then get applied to the real world; it is a mathematical invention that was developed as a way to organize, to mathematize, the world. Starting from a context like market stalls that is already meaningful to the children provides the basis to engage them in this activity of mathematizing. This reverses the way contexts are usually employed in a mathematics lesson: you learn the 'abstract' mathematics and then apply it to a context. As the first lesson on place value shows, this does not necessarily work – the children worked on the abstract but this did not help them apply it. Teachers often say to me that children can understand the mathematics (in the sense of being able to carry out appropriate actions on numerical symbols) but cannot apply it: rather than question the assumption that there is a logical connection in going from the abstract to the application, the implication is that the children are somewhat 'at fault'. As we shall see when I discuss 'situated' learning, research shows that most people's thinking does not work like that. We do not carry around in our heads an abstract 'tool-kit' of mathematical ideas that we open up in appropriate situations. The different activities that we are involved in may invoke different mathematical ideas. Starting from realistic contexts and mathematizing these may help the reapplication of this mathematics to other contexts later.

The careful reader may think that this talk of mathematizing is simply 'discovery' learning in a new guise. It may look similar, but there is a key difference. In coming to mathematize a box of apples into groups of ten I am not suggesting that 'place value' is in the context, waiting for the children to discover it. It is the collective re-creation of the grouping into tens that allows for the emergence of the idea of place value – it is co-constructed through the collective activity rather than 'abstracted' from the context. The sharing of representations and class discussion is crucial here.

Looking at both lessons on place value, by the end of each, the classes had reached similar points (although the second class had only dealt with two-digit numbers rather than going on to three). I'm not claiming that in the second, problem-based lesson, everyone ended up with a clear understanding of place value. But I am claiming that in the second lesson everyone had engaged in some mathematical thinking and problem solving, and was more likely to have developed some insight into the power of place value.

From an outsider's perspective, these two lessons may not look that different. Indeed it may look as though in the second lesson we were letting children 'waste time' in allowing them to record in an inefficient fashion. I do not consider the time spent working 'inefficiently' to have been wasted. Place value was invented to make counting easier so I wanted the children to experience a sense of 'oh, that makes sense, that makes things easier' when they see the power of grouping in tens. And we certainly did not let the children spend an entire lesson working inefficiently only to be shown a better method at the end – that would have been likely to make them feel 'why didn't they show me that earlier?' Engaging the children in this process of mathematizing is why we did not simply show them how to put things in groups of ten at the beginning of the lesson: the process, the activity, is as important as the end.

Examining the different means of mediation in the two lessons tells part of the story but it does not foreground differences in the way the children were interacting with each other, with the teacher and with the mathematics. The activity theorist Yrjö Engström adds to the triadic model of mediated actions three additional elements: rules, community, division of labor – to create a model of an activity system.

In the first lesson the community was predominantly a collection of individuals. Although sitting together for the introduction, there was little interaction between teacher and pupils and none between the pupils themselves. The children then completed the worksheets individually, with more individualization through the worksheets with three-digit numbers available for early finishers. The division of labor in this lesson was based around the teacher explaining the mathematical idea and the children then practicing this. Rules included treating mathematics as a set of conventions that apply to numerals.

Turning to the second lesson, we were working toward a different form of community, a co-operative collective rather than a collection. This entailed a different division of labor with the teacher and I coordinating the collective, moving in and out of whole-class and paired work. The rules beginning to be fostered included treating mathematics as the result of the processes of mathematizing situations rather than as a pre-determined body of knowledge.

In summary I am suggesting that the planning for and structuring of the first lesson was primarily focused on actions: children filling in worksheets and recording the different values of digits. Embedding the second lesson in the narrative context of organizing quantities into groups of ten implicitly recognized the historical development of place value, its social and cultural origins and created an activity system rather than a collection of separate actions.

No-one is alone

Activity theory suggests that even when on one's own, any action is still embedded within the socio-cultural-historical. Lying alone in bed at night silently running over my tables is, in this theoretical sense, not something that I am doing on my own (even though I am physically literally on my own). The thinking that I am engaged in is a result of my socio-cultural-historical circumstances. Although no others are physically present I am still part of the broader ongoing activity of learning my tables in that this night-time practice could contribute to and be part of the history of my performance on a following day's test.

This shift to looking at activity rather than actions is important in challenging the discourse of blame that implicitly characterizes much talk about learning mathematics. Bemoaning the fact that Jimmy or Jenny still have not learnt their tables is lodged in the discourse of actions: they have not put in enough effort or are not motivated enough. The engine of learning is firmly located within the individual who needs to stoke it up more. From an activity perspective, at the very least, one would say that they had not learnt their tables *yet*. But over and beyond that it means looking at the totality of the activity systems within which Jimmy or Jenny is located.

This is not to shift the blame from the individual to the social: 'Jimmy's parents don't value schooling' or 'Jenny's teacher has labeled her as a slow learner' no more account for them not knowing their tables than locating the cause within the individual child. One of the challenges of an activity focus is that the totality of the activity cannot, and should not, be reduced to its separate elements. Lois Holzman in her interpretation of the work of Vygotsky as a performative psychology (that activity between humans is a form of performance) argues for being clear about the difference between distinguishing learners from their context and treating them as separate from the context.

> While we surely can be (and are, in Western cultures) distinguished from the environment, this does not mean we are separate from it. Instead of two separate entities ... there is but one, the unity 'persons-environment'. In this unity, the relationship between persons and environment is complex and dialectical: environment 'determines' us and yet we can change it completely (changing ourselves in the process, since the 'it' – the unity 'persons-environment' – includes us, the changers).
>
> (Holzman 2000: 86)

Two analogies illustrate this difference between separateness and distinction. The first is that of soup and soup-bowls. Here the learner is likened to the soup and the bowl is the context the learning takes place in. The learner is 'held' in a context just as the soup is held in the bowl. Changing the bowl can change the behavior of the soup (for example in a shallow bowl the soup will cool quickly, 'behaving' differently from soup in a tall insulated container) but soup and bowl are quite separate. Changing the soup from tomato to mushroom won't alter the bowl, nor will pouring the soup from a plastic bowl to porcelain change it from broth to consommé. Analogously if learners are separate from their contexts, then schooling can change the 'behavior' of learners but the learner herself is left intact.

Holzman is pointing to a different relationship, more like the classic optical illusion image of two faces and/or a vase. The faces can be distinguished from the vase just as the vase can be distinguished from the face, but neither can be separated from the other; you cannot remove the vase and leave the face nor vice versa. And change one (vase or face) and the other changes: they are dialectically related. From a position of collective activity over individual action, then, teaching has to have collective activity at its core, not simply as a nicety that makes for a more pleasant classroom.

Two heads are better

A focus on the individual rather than collective holds to the popularly held view that if children are working in pairs and one of them is achieving more highly in maths, then the lower achieving child might be brought up to the level of their partner through working together. However, the more capable partner doesn't gain that much from the interaction. This view is often also behind the arguments for setting: the 'bright child' won't gain as much in a mixed-ability class as their thinking won't be 'stretched'. Research shows, however, that paired work raises the level of attainment for both children (Howe and Mercer 2007).

Why might this be? Surely the sum of what a pair can do is simply that – the sum. Putting together a 2 kg stone on a weighing scale with a 3 kg stone can only result in 5 kg. But children are not stones – they interact with each other and in doing so can attain a level of activity that would not be possible on their own. The lesson *Jellybeans* (adapted from Fosnot & Dolk, 2001) with a class of six- and seven-year-olds demonstrates this.

These solutions methods, and those of other children, were not predicted. I had not planned to use the notation that morning that Beth and Ben used, but it turned out to be a 'good offering'. We knew the children well enough to know that the difficulty of the problem meant that no one in class would have been able to solve the problem alone and the origins of the solutions cannot be reduced to an account of the understandings of individual children. The whole lesson was based on the processes of co-construction. And the challenge is considerably harder than what might usually be expected of children of this age.

Jellybeans

The lesson started with a discussion about the idea of equal. I put up on the board

$$25 + 10 = 15 + 10 + 10$$

I asked the children to decide in pairs whether they thought this was true or not. The class were all agreed that it was not true: 25 + 10 makes 35 not 15. Asked about the +10 + 10 that followed after the 15 the children responded that these were not relevant (one child suggested that the board had not been cleaned properly). Like many children of this age they had internalized the idea that the equals sign means 'makes' and that what immediately followed it had to be the answer.

I talked about how the three numbers to the right could be added, representing this by adding them pair wise, 15 + 10 and 25 + 10 by drawing lines down from the 15 and 10 and recording 25 below and then drawing a line down from the 25 and second 10 with the 35 below (Figure 2.1).

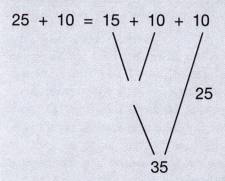

Figure 2.1 Why 25 + 10 = 15 + 10 + 10

continued . . .

Amid groans that I had (again) tried to 'trick' them, there was a general agreement that the statement was true. My recording stayed on the board for the rest of the lesson.

I then set up the main problem for the lesson. I talked about visiting a friend, Richard, who ran a sweet shop and how he had posed a problem that he hoped the children would help him with. He kept jars of different flavors of jellybeans from which he made up orders. I asked for suggestions as to the flavors of beans he might have, in the expectation that the children may have seen the Harry Potter movies and come up with some 'exotic' flavors. But they stuck with traditional fruit flavors, so I added in fish and broccoli. The six flavors were listed on the board and the number of beans there were of each flavor:

Strawberry	72
Orange	23
Apple	33
Cherry	16
Fish	80
Broccoli	72

The problem was that Richard had an order for 300 beans and did not know if he had enough beans in total. Were the children able to find out?

There was a general murmuring of this being hard, but this was the second year of working with the children and they had come to accept and trust us that we would give them challenging problems to work on but that they would get there in the end. In particular, good habits for working in pairs had been established, including sharing one piece of paper. The children also knew that they could use any of the practical materials in the room and record their working in whatever way they found helpful.

A few pairs got out base-ten blocks to model the problem practically but most stuck with paper and pencil. Here are the solutions of two pairs that are typical of the sorts of approaches the children took.

Figure 2.2 shows the work of Amy and Ali. They started copying down the numbers in the order in which they were on the board, but then started adding them systematically. They began with the largest pair, 80 and 72, adding these through the coordinated actions of Amy counting on in tens from 72 and Ali keeping track of the number of tens added on until he reached 80 and Ali reached 152. Both children put out fingers to keep track of action and keep their counting in time with each other.

To add on the second 72 they turned to using the empty number line, then drawing further number lines to add on 33, 23 and 16 in that order.

continued . . .

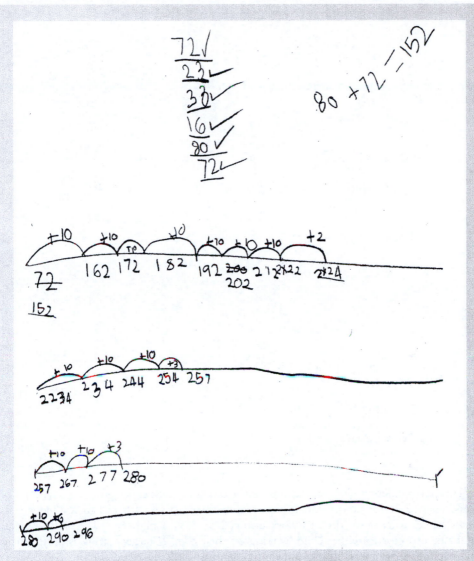

Figure 2.2 Amy and Ali's working

Figure 2.3 shows the work of Beth and Ben. Like Amy and Ali they started by copying down the list of numbers, ticking off 80 but then could not decide what to do next. Ben suggested writing the numbers down as tens and ones and they wrote the tens out, in the same order but horizontally, ticking them off as they went. It was not clear who chose to record the pair-wise addition of the tens by appropriating the 'pull-down' notation that was on the board from the introductory activity. Adding the units mentally, they found the total of the tens and units.

continued . . .

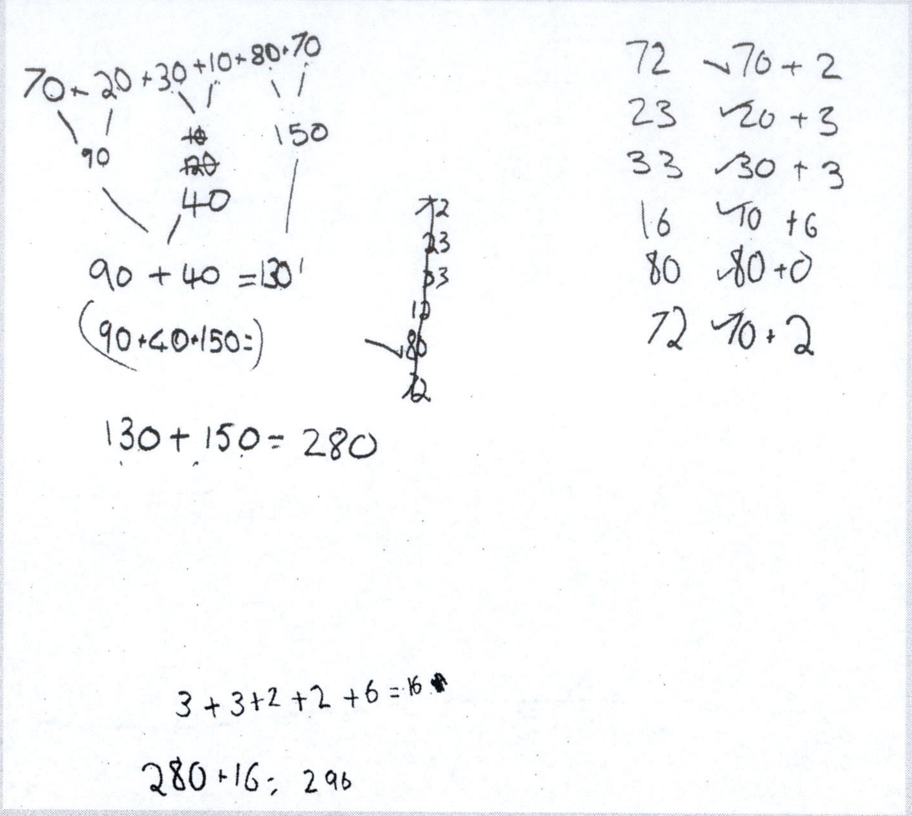

Figure 2.3 Ben and Beth's working

This puts a different gloss on the importance of having high expectations. These expectations need to be for classes and groups within these classes rather than for individuals. Tasks set for pairs of children to work on need to be at a higher level of difficulty than might be expected for either child working on their own. If target setting is only done at the level of expectations for the individual then standards expected for the class may be set too low. Paradoxically, if pairs are not expected to 'stretch' beyond what they can do individually, then it may be that paired work depresses standards rather than raises them.

Historical context

I mentioned earlier that activity theory not only attends to the cultural and social aspects of learning but to the historical. This need not be the 'grand' history of where a lesson is in the history of schooling; it can be the local history of particular classes. It is important to also consider how the history of the children working on the jellybeans problem contributed to their activity.

Aspects of the historical context to note are the artifacts and tools that the children were able to employ. They were familiar with base-ten blocks. We had worked on fluency in adding multiples of ten, and emphasized the strategy of starting with the largest number when adding two numbers. We had introduced the children to the empty number line and had worked with it long enough for this to be a 'model for' addition for most of the children to work with (Gravemeijer 1999).

But in addition to these 'cognitive' tools I want to make links to play and performance and the history of this that we had established, as I consider this to be central to the children 'buying into' a problem that had a level of challenge beyond anything they had met before.

Becker (2000) in his analysis of jazz improvisation argues for the importance of having 'a real shared interest in getting the job done' (p. 175). The considerable time spent at the beginning of the lesson setting the context for the problem encouraged a general 'suspension of disbelief' and getting 'buy-in' from the children. This is not mere speculation: in the early part of setting up the problem one of the girls repeatedly whispered to her neighbor 'It's not true you know. He doesn't really have a friend with a shop.' This increasingly became a stage whisper obviously intended to be overheard by everyone, so I stopped and we spent some time talking about whether it mattered if the 'story' was real or not. Although some of the children were disappointed that I would not reveal the truth, they were generally content to 'play along'. Such 'playing along' helps, I suggest, in the children being willing to 'play' with a problem. This is in contrast to some views that 'artificial' problems do more harm than good. While I would agree that the 'quick' word problem about shopping, followed by another about 'cooking', does discourage engagement, I think more use could be made of more extended narrative scenarios to hook children in.

Groups learn

I once heard an inspector tell of visiting a secondary school and overhearing a teacher comment at her surprise that the test results from a colleague's class were higher than for her class: surprising given that she had the top set and her colleague the second set. Her colleague was then surprised but for a different reason – she thought she had been teaching the top set.

Traditionally, differences like this have been put down to teacher expectations. If you think you are teaching the top set then you will have higher expectations of them, which the class then 'rise' to. And while there is no doubt of the impact of teacher expectations, there is evidence now that such effects can come about from factors beyond the influence of particular teachers, in particular the impact of different group identities that we each adopt.

In much the same way that activity theorists are talking about learning as being more than the sum of individuals' actions, the language of identities is being extended to include groups as well as individuals. I have a vivid memory from my own schooling of the power of collective identity and how this could change. I passed my 11-plus exam and went to the local grammar school. I was quickly inducted into the school's culture of politeness, down to standing when the teacher walked in and doffing my cap to teachers in the street. My form was a model class, displaying no difficult behaviors with any of the teachers. Then in the second year, we had a new history teacher, rather unfortunately, Mr. Askew. He was clearly inexperienced and nervous and within the space of two or three lessons we had turned into the class from hell. (I still mentally blush at the memory of the squashed pear incident.) What was remarkable was how this new collective behavior simply emerged. There were no obvious ringleaders who started off the bad behavior that the rest of us picked up on. Just like a dog sniffing out fear, it was the class that behaved badly, not the sum of the individuals.

Researchers are looking at the interplay between the identities individual learners develop and the identities of the groups to which they belong. The evidence shows that the view that individuals have about their identity as a member of a group can have a real impact on individual learning outcomes. For example, a study in Italy worked with a group of women who were given a maths test. Before taking the test, half of the women discussed the (spurious) fact that gender differences exist in mathematical performance. These women not only performed worse than the other half, the control group, but also reported experiencing more negative thoughts about maths during the course of the test (Cadinu, Maass *et al.* 2005).

Similar results have been shown for other cultural identifications: 'black' boys perform worse when attention is subtly drawn to their racial heritage, while Asian girls perform better (Haslam, Salvatore *et al.* 2008). Such research all points to a similar finding: that the groups you identify with can have powerful impacts – positive and negative – on performance. Many of these studies use maths as the test instrument, so although not about learning mathematics itself they do point to the impact on mathematics attainment. And while they have been carried out in secondary schools my experience leads me to believe that the same effect occurs in primary schools.

It's not fanciful to attribute learning to groups as well as individuals. In the staffroom when, over coffee, teachers talk about, say, the current year 4 being different from last year any differences are not simply a result of it being a different group of children that have come together. Schools, year-groups, classes, do all develop group 'identities' which are more than the sum of the individual identities that the children bring to the group. We have all attached the labels 'difficult', 'bright', and 'lively' to classes as well as pupils. But such group identities need not be fixed, or even constant within short time frames.

Summary

In this chapter I have argued that although the actions of individuals are important in learning, attending to those only tells part of the story. We need to move our attention from planning lessons that focus on the actions of the individuals in the class and the mediating tools and artifacts that will be used to support their activities. We need also to think about the entire activity that the collective is going to be engaged in. This involves thinking about how we encourage a classroom community that is a co-operative collective rather than a collection of individuals. How we think about the division of labor and what rules, particularly about what it means to be engaged in mathematical activity, are in place. These themes are discussed further in Chapters 7 and 8.

Further reading

Vygotsky and Pedagogy by Harry Daniels. While nothing can replace reading a good translation of Vygotsky directly, we must remember that he was writing in a particular time and place and that his work has subsequently been re-interpreted and developed. Daniels's book provides an overview of current thinking on the implications of Vygotsky and what the implications of this might be for classrooms and teaching.

Schools for Growth by Lois Holzman. A great little book that looks at putting Vygotsky's theories into practice in innovative schools in America and Russia.

Chapter 3

Thinking about curriculum

> Abandon the notion of subject-matter as something fixed and ready-made in itself, outside the child's experience; . . . see [experience] as something fluent, embryonic, vital; and we realize that the child and the curriculum are simply two limits which define a single process.
>
> (Dewey 1956)

There was an advert for gas on British TV a few years ago that extolled how 'good' it feels to 'be in control'. Being in control is a popular twenty-first-century myth. Since our lives are no longer in the lap of the gods or fate we want to control them, not only in the here and now but in the future: just look at the prevalence of insurance to cover all sorts of possibilities that might lead to lack of control (over health, heating supply, even burial) (Giddens 1991). Clearly there are many aspects of my life over which I do have control. I like being in control of the level of heat in my house and I have control over the thermostat, which in turn controls the boiler. Some aspects of life are controllable in this way, but they are largely those aspects to which we have found technological solutions.

Much of the discourse around teaching primary mathematics presents it as something that teachers can carefully control. Lessons have to begin by specifying what is to be learnt (WALTs are very popular – We Are Learning Today) and children informed of the success criteria (WILFs: What I Am Looking For). A kernel of sense lies in these practices. There was a time when it was thought good practice not to let the children in on the secret of what they were learning in mathematics; either this would spoil the joy of discovery, or, if they knew that they were doing maths, then they would 'switch off'. It is important that children have awareness of what they are learning. The difficulty is when raising children's awareness turns into fossilized practices; routines you go through but without them having very much meaning. Does children writing down 'today we are learning to solve problems' really help them in problem solving? (My main memory of primary school is about writing the date down. I can understand why knowing when a piece of work was done can be helpful, but why did teachers get into such a snit if you didn't underline it properly?) As I argued in Chapter 1, if teaching were a technological problem, then we would be able to control the learning, but it is an adaptive challenge.

Part of thinking we can control learning comes from hindsight. Looking at lessons that successfully unfold it is easy to assume that they were carefully pre-planned to turn out that way. Keith Sawyer refers to this as 'script-think: the tendency to think that events are more predictable than they really are (Sawyer 2007: 23). One aspect that is particularly prone to 'script-think' in education is the predictability of the order of learning.

Learning is not linear

Two streams of research from King's College, London, both looked at children's learning and its relationship to what they were taught. The Children's Mathematical Frameworks (CMF) examined mathematics lessons over time and in particular how children's understandings changed as teaching sequences went from informal mathematics to formal. Other research by Hazel Denvir and Margaret Brown looked at mapping out networks of children's learning and how this could inform one-to-one teaching. We might expect that it is easier to control learning outcomes in a one-to-one setting than with a class of 30, so I shall look at Hazel and Margaret's findings before comparing these with those of the CMF project.

Diagnostic teaching

Hazel worked with a number of young children to build up a detailed network of concepts and skills in learning early number – from simple one-to-one correspondence to being able to add or subtract pairs of two-digit numbers. She built up the network of understanding through reviewing the extant research and also by interviewing children on a variety of number-based tasks, for example being able to count forwards or back, put numbers in order and solve numerical problems. She constructed the network of connections in a top-down fashion: by looking at the most difficult things that the children could do, she identified the easier skills and knowledge that were also in place. The resulting hierarchy was semi-structured: some items were clearly pre-requisites for later understanding whereas others might be easier than but not necessary for later understanding (Denvir and Brown 1986a).

The network of understanding that Hazel thus built up proved to be a useful model for assessing children's understanding: interviews with another group of children showed that their understandings broadly fitted the levels and connections in the hierarchy. But the network proved less helpful as a guide to what to teach children. Based on their detailed assessments, Hazel was able to identify what, according to the network, appeared to be the most appropriate items of understanding to focus on next with individual children – things that were the next level up and strongly connected to their existing understandings. After this focused teaching, Hazel assessed the children again and was surprised at what she found. While some of the children had learnt the things that she had focused upon, many of them had not. All the children had learnt a variety of things, but many of the things they had learnt seemed to have little or no connection with the items Hazel had targeted through her teaching (Denvir and Brown 1986b).

In the light of this unpredictability, Hazel decided not to try and closely match the teaching to prior learning. Instead, she challenged the children to learn things that, according to her network, should have been too difficult to learn on the basis of their current understandings. In the post-teaching assessments this time round several of the children had learnt these much more difficult ideas (and much more beside these) but even those who had not had achieved the high-level target had 'filled-in' many of the understandings needed on the way to the target idea.

Children's mathematical frameworks

The CMF study was a major piece of research carried out at King's College, London, involving several researchers (Hart, Johnson *et al.* 1989). Although a few years old now, its findings are still significant and yet seem not that widely known. The overall aim of the research was to look at how children moved from informal, often practical, work on mathematics to the formal, more abstract, ideas. For example, how did they move from measuring and recording the circumferences of circles and their radii into an understanding of pi? Or how did finding the areas of rectangles by counting squares link to the development of the formula length times breadth?

The researchers worked across many schools and classrooms and selected six children from each class that they were studying, two lower attainers, two higher attainers and two average (identified as such by their teachers). The research team interviewed these children on four occasions to explore their understandings of the mathematics to which they were being introduced. One interview was before the beginning of the entire teaching sequence, a second was immediately before the lesson where the formal mathematics was to be introduced, the third soon after this lesson and a fourth interview three months after the teaching. On the basis of the children's responses, the researchers identified what they called the 'rule of thirds'. Across all the different topics and across all the different lessons in all the different schools, at each round of interviews the children fell into one of three groups. Approximately one third of the children had almost no understanding of the formal mathematics, another third had some partial understanding and the final third had good understanding.

Looking into this data the CMF team developed a further insight: the children falling into each third changed, sometimes dramatically, at each interview point. For example, some children actually understood the formal mathematics before the teacher had even begun to teach it, but three months after the teaching no longer understood it. Or a child might display no understanding of the formal mathematics immediately before the lesson nor any immediately after it, but showed full understanding three months later. This suggests that at any point in time, teaching is probably being effective for about a third of the class. So we should not beat ourselves up for not 'matching' the teaching to every child.

Apart from anything else, the CMF research raises questions about when we choose to assess children. In research parlance, the interviews that took place three months after the teaching are 'delayed post-test' assessments and are probably the most revealing of all the interviews. After all there is little point in teaching something if three months later the children show no understanding of it. In classrooms, the most popular time for assessing children is often immediately after a topic has been taught. The CMF research shows this is not a strong predictor of who will still (or will have begun to) understand the mathematics three months later. An assessment project I was involved with was developing assessment items with teachers: some of the teachers were very reluctant to assess children on topics that they had not recently taught. And they were even more resistant to testing the children on things that they had not yet taught, asking what would be the point of that? Again the CMF research shows that some children do come to class with knowledge of mathematics that they have not yet been taught and so it might well be helpful to find out about this.

Taken together Hazel's research and the CMF findings show that the link between teaching and learning is less direct than we imagine it to be. Teaching may prompt learning but teaching cannot control pre-determined outcomes.

Slicing up the curriculum

There's a popular metaphor in time management books around the question 'how do you eat an elephant?' Setting aside the question of why you would want to do this in the first place, the answer provided is 'one slice at a time'. Eating an elephant is an impossible task to do all at once, but any huge task can be accomplished if only it is broken down into small manageable slices. This is a popular view of teaching – slice the mathematics up into manageable 'objectives' and feed them to the children one at a time. That maths appears to lend itself particularly easily to being carved up into small slices makes the metaphor particularly appealing. But in slicing up an elephant have you really eaten an elephant? While literally you would have done so, in another sense what you've eaten is a number of fragments. In 'ingesting' small slices of mathematics (objectives) you might have managed to eat the whole of the curriculum, but may have gained little sense of what mathematics as a unified whole is (any more than plates of elephant slices would provide a sense of elephantness).

Robitaille and Dirks (1982) suggested that we should not talk about the mathematics curriculum as though it is a single thing but that we need to consider the intended curriculum, the implemented curriculum and the attained curriculum. Looking at developments, in England at least, in the intended curriculum helps explain the persistence of the one-slice-at-a-time metaphor.

Intended curriculum

The intended curriculum is, as the name suggests, what somebody, somewhere expects the children to learn in mathematics. When I was a beginning primary school teacher there was no national curriculum (ah, the headiness of it all) and, in theory, the intended curriculum was down to the school or even the individual teacher. In practice there were actually several de facto intended curricula, determined by which textbook scheme your school followed.

All that changed with the introduction of the first national curriculum in England in 1990. Immediate reaction to this first curriculum was that it contained way too much detail: two programmes of study made out of 14 attainment targets each broken down into ten levels of attainment and each of these exemplified by several teaching objectives – well, you can do the maths. Subsequent revisions of the national curriculum reduced the level of detail each time. But the introduction into England of the National Numeracy Strategy brought us back full circle to a level of detail that far exceeded that set out in the first curriculum (Department for Education and Employment (DfEE) 1999).

Implemented curriculum

Teachers have no choice but to plan a sequence of lessons that occur one after the other. As Pete Griffin beautifully puts it: 'Teaching can be seen as taking place in time, while learning takes place over time' (1989).

Faced with a plethora of detailed teaching objectives to deliver and a sense that the curriculum is huge, is it any wonder that the metaphor of eating an elephant appeals? You implement this overwhelmingly detailed curriculum by serving up slices in each lesson.

Attained curriculum

Robitaille and Dirks's original sense of the attained curriculum was to look at what children had actually learned and how this *compared* to the intended and implemented curricula. Recently, however, the discourse has moved to looking at the attained curriculum in terms of whether or not it *matches* the intended. Children are assessed against the intended learning outcomes – what they actually might have learned could be very different but is only of marginal interest.

Blurring the distinction between teaching objectives and (intended) learning outcomes does not help: I can specify what my teaching objective is before a lesson, but I cannot, in most lessons, be that much in control of the learning outcomes (as Hazel Denvir's and the CMF research so powerfully demonstrates). It is like the old joke:

Tom: I taught my dog to talk
Harry: But he only barks
Tom: I only said I taught him, not that he learned.

One of the consequences of specifying the curriculum in such increased detail is that this model for planning teaching starts to be assumed to be the reality of learning. Children are not assessed on what they have learned, but on whether they have learned very specific objectives. Rather than the attained curriculum – in the sense of what the children actually learn – being a guide to help shape further teaching it has become a tick-list. Children's learning in its own right is not valued; it simply is a means of checking out whether the prescribed curriculum has been correctly delivered. Formative assessment, assessment that helps teachers know what children have learned as well as where they need support, is less important than summative assessment to check off the objectives.

We need to be alert not to fall into confusing the map (the intended curriculum) for the terrain (children's learning).

Limiting teaching

Trying to closely pre-specify learning objectives may not match with how children learn and it can also put limits on teaching. First it can make it difficult to attend to what the children bring to the lesson, or result in only paying lip service to it. In a study of the teaching of mental strategies that Tamara Bibby, Jeremy Hodgen and I carried out (Askew, Bibby *et al.* 2002), we observed lessons where children were invited to find answers mentally to calculations and then share their methods with the teacher and class. But if their methods did not fit with those that had been pre-determined for the lesson then these were, at best, judged by the teachers as not relevant to the lesson, rather than being a resource for the class to discuss and build upon. For example, a lesson objective might have been to add a two-digit number by rounding to the nearest ten and adjusting. Adding 37 + 39 according to the teaching objective would be to add 40 and then subtract one.

A child who knew that double 38 was 76 and that this was the correct answer (because one from the 39 onto the 37 would balance out and give the same result) would not have been given the opportunity to share her thinking with the rest of the class.

Another limitation on closely pre-specifying learning outcomes is that it is easy to fall into choosing objectives that (apparently) can easily be controlled. So an objective like 'adding 9 by adding ten and adjusting' lends itself to being pre-specified: it can be broken down into a series of steps, each of these can be modeled by the teacher and children can go off and practice them. But even then there is a difficulty in that this becomes an isolated piece of knowledge extracted from its links and relationships with other aspects of the maths. Most skills in maths only make sense in relation to other ones, so picking them off in isolation isn't the most sensible way to address them.

I reiterate that I am not arguing for an 'anything goes' approach to mathematics teaching – clearly lessons have to be designed with likely learning outcomes in mind. But note the plural here – outcomes – and whether or not a specific outcome will be achieved cannot be predicted at the beginning of a lesson.

If you look at other aspects of learning, then this is not how children come to understand. Children do not learn 'one objective at a time'. They learn to talk, for example, by being immersed in complex environments where they do not initially understand the words, but activities get done: games get played, cakes get baked, clothes get put on. In taking part in these activities at the level that they can, children come to solve the problem of how the others are communicating with each other and in doing so they figure out how to talk. They are engaged in a 'community of practice', involved in the activities of that community and inducted into these over time (Lave and Wenger 1991). As I argue in Chapter 8, we need to examine the classroom mathematical communities and make them enticing for children to want to become part of.

To take another example, look at how children learn to play video games. They start, and continue, by playing the game, figuring out what the rules are as they go and developing the skills to succeed within the game context. They do not practice a set of decontextualized skills, read the game rulebook and then finally get round to playing. Outside of school most learning comes about through engaging in whole activities rather than learning discrete behaviors or actions.

Planning lessons around mathematical activity, rather than individual actions, more closely matches how we 'naturally' come to learn. The fact that school mathematics is more formal and more intentional than learning to talk or play video games does not mean that children suddenly become different types of learners when they walk into the classroom. Reflective teaching needs to focus on the activity, the experience, of the learner, not on the actions of the teacher, as Bernie Neville reminds us:

> I have come to believe that we learn very little by being told the answers to questions we have not asked. It seems to me that learning originates in the experiences of the learner, not those of the teacher. A great deal of what we learn we learn by a sort of absorption, or we just 'pick it up' through experience, as we go along, without the need for teaching. It is only in schools that we abandon this natural way of learning. In schools, we tell children (or adults) things we consider important, and then we expect them to remember what we tell them. I believe we tell them largely in vain. The learning has little to do with our telling.
>
> (Neville 2005: 24)

Knowledge or knowing?

At the base of all this muddling of curriculum, teaching and learning is a view of starting with the mathematics as preformed – the objective for today's lesson is pre-determined. We need to move, in Brent Davis's term, from 'preformed to performed' (Davis 1996). From knowledge – the pre-determined, preformed collection of mathematical 'bits', to knowing – the performing of being mathematical.

The dominance of the discrete, slices, approach to teaching mathematics lies in this difference between talking about knowledge and knowing. The continuing appeal of 'knowledge' is that it can be 'packaged' up into neat pieces (learning objectives) that can be delivered. Knowing, in contrast, places more emphasis on the process rather than the product.

Some skills can be taught in a piecemeal, slice-by-slice style, which is probably one of the reasons why traditional paper and pencil methods are still held so dear by some. They lend themselves to being taught by breaking them down into a discrete set of skills; here are the steps in carrying out the addition algorithm, long multiplication or whatever, now practice them. While there is a place for some skills they are a small part of the mathematics repertoire that children now need.

The continued emphasis on disctrete item of knowledge, rather than activities that lead to knowing, also lies in the persistence of the 'tool-kit' view of learning mathematics. It used to be argued that learning mathematics provided some sort of training for the mind – an hour of maths was the brain equivalent of an hour at the gym. Just as gritting your teeth and enduring the pain and discomfort of lifting weights can build up your biceps, so it was argued that gritting your teeth and enduring the pain of committing to memory a load of mathematical mumbo-jumbo would build up your mental muscles. Mathematics built 'character' – 'I endured Y9 algebra and it never did me any harm'. While the building up of physical strength in the gym may enable you to lift large weights in other contexts, the drilling of mathematical mental muscles does not, in most circumstances, transfer to other contexts.

From research into the brain, it turns out that there may be an element of truth to the fact that mathematical activity (actually any activity) repeated over time does literally change the structure of the brain (Doidge 2007). But that does not mean that you then automatically have a mathematical 'tool-kit' to serve you in any situation. You might get better at doing the mathematics you are presented with in mathematics classrooms: you might be no better at using it elsewhere, as the research into situated learning demonstrates.

Situated learning

We know now that learning is often quite 'situated' – tied to the particular circumstances in which knowledge is gained or used: the circumstances in which we become knowers. Two streams of research in particular, that of Jean Lave and also Terezinha Nunes and her colleagues, have findings that challenge the view that mathematics can simply be 'transferred' in the heads of learners out of the mathematics lesson into other subjects or contexts.

Lave's research into the mathematics of 'just plain folks' (jpf's) as they went about their daily lives revealed the large extent of mathematical thinking in which people did engage, even though they might not have described it as mathematics (Lave 1988). (There is a popular view that the mathematics that people use in their daily lives isn't 'real' mathematics, it is just common sense. Maths is all that stuff that you can't do.) For example, one aspect of mathematics that Lave examined was the everyday use of fractions. Her research subjects were American women and many of them were following diets that required quite precise measuring out of quantities of, say, cottage cheese. The women had good strategies for creating quantities such as ⅔ of ¾ of a pot. However, when Lave presented them with identical calculations but set out as though in a school textbook, the women had difficulty finding the answers to them.

Nunes and colleagues also looked at mathematical activity outside the classroom, researching Mexican teenagers who, outside schooling, worked in markets selling fruit (Nunes, Carraher et al. 1993). These teenagers displayed remarkable facility in mentally calculating total costs and the change that they needed to give buyers but, as in Lave's study, presented with such calculations (using the actual costs and figures that they had been working with in the market) set out as they might encounter them in school, the teenagers struggled to find correct answers. Their difficulties were largely a result of not using the 'rule of thumb' methods that they drew upon in the market but trying instead to recall the methods that they had been taught in school and making errors in these.

Such research, and other, similar, findings, challenges the 'tool-box' metaphor of learning mathematics: that what students learn in the mathematics classroom equips them with a mental 'tool-box' of strategies and techniques that can then be 'transferred' to particular circumstances and the appropriate mathematical 'tool' be selected to apply to the task in hand. The fact that the women in Lave's study did not do this led Lave to argue for the 'situated' nature of learning: that learning is much more context dependent and that we need to examine these assumptions of the 'tool-box' metaphor.

Lave argues further that the continued dominance of the metaphor of 'transferring' is down to the success of the few in education who are able to transfer knowledge across situations: they rise up the educational system and perpetuate this view of learning. Lave argues that, rather than trying to get everyone else to be able to transfer abstract knowledge across contexts, we should acknowledge that the majority of jpf's do not learn in this way and our education system should work with this reality rather than against it.

More recent theoretical developments have looked at the idea of how we all engage in 'communities of practice'. We learn the tacit rules and expectations of the different communities that we are part of and do not automatically draw on these in different contexts. In the case of the Mexican fruit sellers we might argue that the tacit 'rules' of the market placed an emphasis on working mentally, while mathematics classroom 'rules' might include having to show your working with paper and pencil and using the method that the teacher has shown you rather than your own informal methods. The teenagers draw on different 'knowledges' in the different communities.

Jo Boaler's research in secondary schools demonstrates the effectiveness of using a problem-solving-based pedagogy: learners did as well on exams as those following a more traditional curriculum but also reported more use of mathematics outside school (Boaler 1997). If we want children to engage in mathematical activity – outside school – then teaching has to be based around collective problem solving, more closely matching the communities of practice that learners are engaged in outside school.

From one-act dramas to soap operas

Along with the view of teaching as delivering a discrete collection of objectives is the reification of the lesson as the primary unit for thinking about teaching and learning. Cultural differences in thinking about children's misconceptions illustrate this. In Japan, teachers' books provide guidance for developing children's understanding of, say, fractions over a period of time. Part of the guidance deals with the difficulties and misconceptions that children are likely to exhibit over the teaching sequence. The teacher guides are clear that teachers should not expect children's thinking to change quickly away from these misconceptions and that it may take several weeks before children have sorted their thinking out. That is a very different message from one from England's National Numeracy Strategy that suggested that the final ten minute 'plenary' part of a lesson include 'correcting' misconceptions.

One of the lessons that I observed from one of the most successful teachers in the Effective Teachers of Numeracy project (Askew 2010) was about pie charts. The children were finding it difficult to compare charts with different totals. For example, one chart might show that 50 percent of children in a school of 200 chose reading as a favourite pastime, whilst another chart showed that 25 percent of 600 children in another school had chosen reading. When asked in which school had the larger number of children chosen reading, the children could not 'get past' seeing 50 percent as bigger than 25 percent, irrespective of the sample size. The teacher drew this part of the lesson to a close without trying to reach any resolution of the children's confusion. Talking afterwards the teacher explained that he knew there was no point in trying to sort things out there and then and that he needed to think about how he was going to come back to this later. I had not come across it at the time, but research is showing that sleeping on it probably was beneficial to both the teacher and the children.

Sleep on it. It works

There is evidence in the psychology research that the old adage of 'sleeping on it' has a lot of truth to it. The evidence shows that our brains continue to work on problems that have caught our interest while we sleep and that insight occurs the following day without further effort – even without consciously bringing the problems to mind. American adults volunteered to take part in research about learning maths. They were given a sequence of numbers and told the rule for generating successive numbers. The rule was quite complicated and the experiment, as far as the volunteers were concerned, was to see if they could recall the rule the following day. What they did not know was that there was a much simpler rule for figuring out subsequent terms in the series. Returning the following day and asked if they could remember the rule, over 80 percent of the volunteers reported that they had spotted a rule that was much easier to remember. They had not been told to do this. They were not aware of there being a simpler rule. But their minds had worked on this irrespective of being asked to do so (Stickgold and Ellenbogen 2008).

An incident from some research that my colleague Margaret Brown carried out nicely demonstrated this with a child. A researcher working with Margaret was interviewing children about their understanding of measurement and asked one six-year-old if they could use a number of interlocking cubes to measure the height of a cardboard tower. The child could indeed do this, but presented with the more challenging task of using just a single cube to measure the height of a different tower the child indicated that they couldn't. It happened that the interview had to end at that point but there were more questions to ask and so the child agreed to meet with the researcher again the following morning. The researcher picked up the interview from the question about measuring the tower with a single cube. 'You asked me that yesterday,' said the child. 'That's right,' said the researcher, 'can you remember what you said?' 'Yes, I said I couldn't. But I can now.' And indeed she could.

We need to question the current orthodoxy that all mathematical learning can be wrapped up in a neat package of a single lesson. Working on problems, leaving them unresolved at the end of the lesson, and returning to them the following day may be more helpful than getting them 'done and dusted' in one lesson. And rather than one objective following another – a lesson as a series of one-act dramas – we need to have a series of ideas threading through sequences of lessons – as soap operas have multiple story lines.

Summary

Let me be clear. Teachers have a huge influence over learning, but there are limits to that influence. Good teaching recognizes those limitations and works within them. Not recognizing those limitations can lead to the 'blame' culture that I sometimes overhear – 'I don't know, I taught them (insert your favourite mathematical topic in here) yesterday and they've forgotten it today.'

Thinking about how we deal with other forms of learning can point up some of the differences that we think will suddenly happen when children move into a formal learning situation (school). When children are learning to talk, caregivers instinctively know that learning takes time to be well embedded and for children to become fluent. They are patient with the fact that two-year-olds will continue to make mistakes when learning to talk and don't say 'I told you yesterday, it's biscuit, not bikkie'. They accept the idea (although they may not call it this) of working within the child's 'zone of proximal development' and playing with the language and accepting that the child contributes what they can and that the more experienced other 'completes' the activity.

Therein lies one of the biggest difficulties in teaching mathematics – the assumption that what the child brings is not significant, or that they do not have anything to bring to the activity. Part of that comes from being too tightly wedded to the 'topic' or learning outcome of the lesson. In conversation with young children, there is joint negotiation of the shaping and direction of the conversation. The child as much determines where a conversation 'goes' as does the adult. The conversation is jointly owned. How much mathematics in classrooms is jointly owned?

Further reading

Educating Psyche by Bernie Neville. Drawing on mythology, Neville provides an engaging look at how teaching might tap into the power of the brain for 'off-line' learning.

The Brain That Changes Itself by Norman Doidge. Neuroscience is, I think, a long way from providing insights into what we actually need to do in class, but it is challenging some long-held beliefs about how we learn. This is one of many popular science books that examine current understandings of the brain.

Chapter 4

Thinking about teaching

It is impossible to know reality for the same reason that makes it impossible to sing potatoes; they may be grown, or pulled, or eaten, but not sung. Reality has to be 'been'.

(Bion 1984)

Writing about teaching and learning is a bit like trying to 'sing' potatoes. Teaching and learning are experiences that we live through – any written account of these experiences can only be a shadow of the real thing. In moving from lived experience to describing it we commonly take metaphors from elsewhere to help our thinking: teacher as gardener, as musical conductor, as midwife. Teaching is teaching: do we need to compare it to something else in order to understand it? (Do surgeons understand their profession by likening it to, say, flower arranging?)

The writers Lakoff and Johnson (1980) suggest that much, if not most, of our language is metaphorical and that we make sense of abstract ideas by linking them to physical activity. Look at how we talk about our emotional states – feeling 'up', feeling 'down' – there are echoes of the literal physical positions we find ourselves in when healthy or ill (or 'under the weather'). Teaching is a complex activity and we resort to metaphors to describe and make sense of it. Metaphors, by their nature, emphasize some aspects and play down others. Is teaching like gardening, with children small plants and flowers that the teacher has to water and nurture to help them bloom in the kindergarten (children garden)? Or is teaching similar to erecting a building that requires putting up 'scaffolding' to hold it up until it can support itself?

The metaphor of 'scaffolding' is popular – a structure that supports what is being 'constructed' – isn't that what teaching is all about? A research project that my colleagues Joan Bliss and Sheila Macrae and I carried out examined what scaffolding might look like in practice (1996). It turned out that it was a slippery thing: anything that we observed that might be described as scaffolding could just as easily have been labeled 'teaching'. Thinking further about the metaphor of scaffolds, they support but they also constrain and direct the style and direction of a building. They rely on blueprints, the plan has already determined what will be constructed and so limits creativity (which of course fits with the myth of teaching controlling learning that I talked about in the previous chapter). That's the problem with metaphors – they can limit our thinking as well as open it up. In this chapter I look at various metaphors and theories about teaching primary mathematics, their strengths and limitations, and how they can help us think about transforming it.

Keeping it all on track

'Track' is a metaphor that we use a lot in talking about teaching and learning. Are the children on track? How best to keep track of their learning? Beware of getting sidetracked in a lesson. The origins of the tracks metaphor lie in the journey metaphor and in particular from the laying down of tracks for railways. It's a powerful and seductive metaphor. Train journeys are direct and usually quite swift. Trains are more rarely diverted or caught up in 'jams' than cars are. If my goal is to get from A to B smoothly and directly, trains are a good option. If I want the children to learn, say, long multiplication, getting them on the right track and taking through the various steps (stops or stations) along this track sounds like an effective and efficient way of teaching. But the tracks metaphor breaks down in several places (goes off the rails?). First of all, train drivers only have to get one train at a time from A to B: teachers are driving a whole class of little trains (some say teaching is like herding cats). Most importantly, children, unlike trains, have free will. Trains don't come up with alternative suggestions about how to get to the destination. Trains, once powered up, don't need convincing that the tracks they are on are worth traveling along.

If teaching is like any sort of journey then I suggest it is more like sailing than train travel. Both forms of transport are similar in that they involve getting from A to B. A train route looks the same both before and after the event – looking forward you can see where the tracks head towards, looking back you can see where they came from. Getting from A to B when sailing is not nearly so predictable as so many things are outside your control, depending on the wind speed and direction. A skilled sailor will reach her destination. But it might be sooner or later than she expected, and she will not have been able to precisely predict the route taken. After the event, knowing what the conditions were, she can re-construct how the route emerged. And the next time she makes that journey, this knowledge will inform her decisions, but no two sailing experiences will ever be the same, just as no two lessons are ever the same.

Teaching and learning is somewhat mysterious and unpredictable and we need to accept and work with that rather than behave as though it were completely controllable by keeping it on the track. By pretending it is entirely within our control we set ourselves up either for dull mathematics lessons or for frustration. Like sailing, in teaching you start out with a particular direction (learning outcome) in mind and as the lesson unfolds so it becomes clear that a detour must be made, or the children come up with something that might be a more valuable or interesting place to explore.

A key difference here is between complicated and complex systems: train driving is complicated, sailing is complex.

Complicated or complex?

System, complicated, complex: words like this get used in everyday talk but I'm using them in a particular way here so a few definitions are in order.

Being systematic, the schooling system, a hot water system, the office filing system: the popular use of system is either to describe a set of things that are connected or that operate together, or as a way of doing things. I will be using it in the former sense of things operating together and the important and significant distinction between complicated systems and complex systems. To explore the distinction I'm drawing on two other metaphors: clocks and clock restoring, and gardens and gardening.

Complicated systems

My uncle was a keen clock restorer and liked nothing better than taking old pendulum clocks apart, cleaning all the cogs and restoring the clock. I could never see how he could spot the differences between the cogs when they were all laid out on the table, as they all looked the same to me. Clock restoring is a complicated business. It is complicated in a particular sense of the word in that clocks are highly predictable systems. A clock is, in the literal sense of the phrase, the sum of its parts. Left to its own devices a wind-up clock will not turn into a battery-operated one or into a transistor radio (bear with me, the point of this will become clear). The different parts of a clock interact with each other but they don't actually change each other (except in the mechanical way of parts physically wearing each other down). Most importantly, in the sense in which they are labeled complicated, clocks are highly predictable systems. This predictability follows the logic of 'if-then'. If a pendulum clock is running fast or slow, then adjusting the weight of the pendulum has a predictable effect on the time keeping. Particular actions determine particular, predictable, results – a key feature of complicated systems.

Complex systems

Gardens, like clocks, have a number of components – flora and fauna – all of which interact with each other. Unlike the cogs of a clock, however, the parts of a garden change significantly as a result of these interactions: insects pollinating plants affect the growth of the plants, which in turn affects the insect population. Feedback loops are set in motion and, over time, gardens change and can become dramatically different. They may flourish or they may wither, or parts of them may thrive whilst others do not. The changes that occur in a garden are not random: cause-and-effect does operate. The big difference is that the effects of particular actions are much harder, if not impossible, to predict in the same way that we can predict the effect of changes to a clock's mechanism. Chopping down a bush may allow others nearby to flourish or it may upset the local eco-system such that nearby plants suffer. The action may even have an impact way beyond the boundaries of that particular garden. This is the origin of the 'butterfly effect' metaphor: that a butterfly flapping its wings in Japan may trigger a tornado in America. A gardener can make an educated guess as to the effect of her actions, but unlike the clock restorer, she cannot accurately pre-determine the impact. Gardens are typical examples of complex systems. They involve multiple feedback loops that dynamically change the whole structure. In complex systems, the results of actions *depend* upon the actions carried out, but they do not uniquely determine them.

We have a strong belief (wish?) in teaching as complicated system, in that we would like to know how to control it better, on the assumption that the system works along the 'if-then' lines of logic. Teaching 'tips' that claim that 'if-you-do-such-and-such-then-this-will-happen' are eagerly sought. That there are some tactics that appear to operate in this way – see 'Count to five' – encourages the search and hope for more 'if-thens' to solve the problems of teaching.

The trouble is that there are not that many 'if-thens' and, as Michael Fullan points out (2003), the failure of 'if-then' leads to 'if-only' talk. 'Well, I explained it the way the book said but they didn't get it' has the implicit '*If* you teach it this way *then* the children are certain to learn it.' Popular such statements include:

'If only they paid more attention then . . .'
'If only they weren't the bottom set, then . . .'
'If only they had remembered last year's lessons then . . .'
'If only [insert your own favourite phrase here] then . . .'

Rather than fall into the trap of 'if . . . only' talk we can reframe how we talk and think about teaching and accept that the link between teaching and learning is not as direct as we would wish. Teaching and learning is a complex system: learning is dependent upon teaching but cannot be completely determined by it.

Accepting this complexity is liberating. It means teachers accept things as they are and work from that reality, rather than wish that things were different. It is easy within the complicated 'if . . . then' mindset to think that certain things are not possible because certain pre-requisites are not in place. For example, when I first went to work with one particular school, the model of teaching did not involve very much pupil discussion. It was the case that the children were not very articulate, but talking and listening to the teachers it became clear that there was some implicit 'if only . . . then' reasoning behind the lack of talk in mathematics lessons: 'if only these children were more articulate then we could ask them to talk about maths'. The danger with such reasoning is that it does not challenge or try to change the current situation. If the children are not very articulate then what is going to happen to change that? Rather than accept this situation as limiting we need to ask what could be done to change it. Holding true to believing that talk is central in learning mathematics (as I do) means promoting this in classrooms whatever the level of competency the children bring.

This view of teaching and learning as a complex system is why you will not find any cast-iron guarantees in this book for how to solve the problems of teaching primary mathematics. What I hope you do find are some insights from research and experience that encourage you to question what you take for granted in teaching and learning mathematics, and to make some changes, to try things out and to see whether your class flourishes or not.

On the surface the teacher wait time research looks like a classic example of if-then results: if you pause then more children will talk. But of course it is not that pausing

Count to five

One of the few educational research findings that does show predictable outcomes arising from specific actions is the research on 'teacher wait' time. Studies of classrooms show that most of the time someone is talking in a classroom and most of that time it is the teacher. Along the classic 80/20 split, 80 percent of the time there is talk in a classroom and 80 percent of that time it is the teacher talking. Wait time studies look at the effect of teachers asking a question and then pausing before either re-phrasing the question or saying something else. Simply pausing and silently counting to five has been demonstrated, many times over, to dramatically alter the balance of talk – much more of the talk then comes from the children and much less from the teacher (Tobin 1986).

actually *causes* the children to talk more (in the way that hitting a billiard ball with a cue causes the ball to move). If that were the case then logically it should follow that pausing for even longer would cause even more pupils' talk (just as striking the ball more firmly makes it travel further). It doesn't: pauses that are too long actually reduce the children to silence. The pausing itself does not cause the talk. While a pause gives the children more time to think, the pausing, perhaps more importantly, creates a different set of expectations and relations in the class, ones where children feel their contributions are genuinely being sought and so they begin to offer them.

Teaching for complexity

Accepting classrooms as complex systems requires us to face up to the fact that, much as we would like it, it is a myth that as a teacher I can closely predict and control what a class of children are going to learn. While we cannot control learning directly, we can shape the experiences within which learning can occur and, as I shall argue throughout this book, the role of the teacher is to optimize these opportunities and in doing so maximize the likelihood of learning.

The conundrum in trying to focus on learning is that all we can ever observe are actions within activity. I have had teachers say to me 'I know Meg understands multiplication but she cannot use it in problems.' In what sense does that mean that she does actually understand multiplication? To be able to carry out a multiplication calculation is one thing, to be able to apply it is, for me, one of the tests of understanding. I begin to think that children have learnt something if they can begin to use it, play with it in a slightly different way from what I've set up. But this judgment always has to be speculative – a conjecture – as they might soon encounter a situation where they do not bring their knowledge to bear. Is that a result of lack of understanding? My reaction to that is that it is my duty to help them expand their repertoire of where to apply and use particular skills and knowledge. I accept that there is always a growing edge to understanding, which is a positive position to work from rather than thinking 'oh they never really understood it' or 'they've forgotten it again'.

In claiming that we cannot control learning, I am not suggesting that teachers have no role. I do believe we can challenge, provoke, encourage, spark, ignite, or rouse learning. We can help children examine, acknowledge, reflect on and review what they have learned. But I cannot predict that all of this will happen in the space of a 50-minute lesson and that everyone will reach the same destination at the end of the lesson.

Scale independence

Complex systems are 'scale-independent': zoom in on part of a complex system and it bears a similarity to a wider view (Davis, Sumara *et al.* 2000). Fractals are the archetypical example here: enlarge part of a fractal and it looks similar to the bigger picture. This property does not hold true for other mathematical figures. Zoom in on part of, say, a triangle, and it does not look like a whole triangle. The natural world contains many things that have this complex, self-similar property: individual spears of broccoli are similar to whole heads; coast-lines viewed from a satellite look similar to close-up views of specific beaches. Complexity theorists suggest that this self-similarity property also applies to individuals and collectives. For example, as we will see in Chapter 8, how small groups in classrooms work together – cooperatively or competitively – is likely to be mirrored in how the larger collective of the class works together.

Brent Davis and Elaine Simmt (2003) argue there are two separate aspects that we consider in teaching: there is the 'canonical' mathematics content, which historically developed over many years, and the 'local' learning of individuals and classes. We tend to see these as two very different types of knowledge but Davis and Simmt argue that these are more similar than different. Extending the language of learning beyond the heads of individuals, they argue that we can think of mathematics itself as having learned over the centuries. Just as there is a time when the child has no knowledge of place value and over the course of their personal history comes to know of it, so too there was a time when mathematics had no knowledge of place value (it had not been invented by mathematicians) and over time the discipline came to 'know' place value. The difference, Davis and Simmt argue, between the individual learner coming to know place value and the discipline of mathematics coming to know it is one of scale. This loops us back to activity as having an historical dimension to it, as opposed to actions in the here and now. A focus on activity directs us to attend to process, actions to products.

The two 'place value' lessons from Chapter 2 exemplify what I think is one of the central difficulties with primary maths: the attention to manipulating symbols – products – rather than processes that led to these products. The symbols represent (as in 'stand in for') mathematical activity. They are not the activity itself. Yet we become so familiar with talking about the activity as though it were in the symbols that we lose this distinction. There aren't 3 tens in 35 because we write a 3 and a 5, it's because of the activity of organizing unstructured collections of objects into groups of ten that the notation follows. From a cultural, historical activity approach to place value the children come to appreciate how grouping in tens is a way of organizing objects to make counting them more manageable, not simply be able to say that the 3 in 35 'stands for' 3 tens. There is a double payoff here – not only were the children learning about how place value works, they were also learning about why it developed and why it is of central importance in mathematics. Place value, and by extension mathematics, is not something to do with manipulating symbols or something that you do in school to get praise from the teacher; it is, in Vygotsky's terms, a cultural tool to do things with.

Through working on the problem of Jo's bowls of fruit, place value was initially introduced as a physical tool – a way of organizing a collection of objects to make counting them easier. As the children become familiar and confident in doing this, so the idea became one that they could think with – you no longer need to organize the 43 apples into groups of ten to know that there are four groups of ten. To adults who are very familiar with this notation system, it can all seem so obvious as to be trivial but looking at the history of mathematics it took many centuries for place value to become the accepted form of notation. If we want to put 87 apples into bags of 10 then we know that we can create 8 with 7 apples left over. By comparison, a Roman marketer with a box of LXXXVII apples has to do quite a bit of mental juggling to get to the same conclusion. You cannot really think with the Roman numeral system in the way that we can think with the place value system (and the fact that it all seems so obvious to us is hiding the fact that we are thinking with the system). I return to the importance of tools for thinking with in Chapter 10.

This example goes to the heart of one of the arguments for a problem-solving pedagogy that is central to this book. We were working on place value through the context of market stalls not so that the children would be able to solve similar problems later (although they may be able to). Nor is the maths in context to make it more 'interesting' to the children, more linked to their lives outside school. We were using the context, the practical solving of the problem, to help the children appreciate the power of the mathematics. Mathematics, like language, is a tool for thinking with and that has to be its primary purpose in the curriculum. Problem solving acts as a springboard for mathematical activity and thinking.

Effective teachers of numeracy

A project that Margaret Brown, Valerie Rhodes and other colleagues and I conducted set out to find out what made some teachers more effective at teaching numeracy than others (Askew, Brown *et al.* 1997). Working with 90 teachers and detailed case studies of 18 of these teachers we judged effectiveness by how much improvement the children in their classes showed on a specific test that we set them toward the beginning and end of the school year. We looked at various factors that might have accounted for why some classes had higher average gains on our test than others did.

Not all of our findings fitted with some of the commonly held beliefs about what makes a teacher effective. For example, across our sample we observed some teachers with a preferred style of whole-class teaching, some who used group work most of the time and some who largely set individual work. No single style of class organization for mathematics teaching predicted how effective a teacher was. Our findings also challenged assumptions about the sort of mathematical qualifications that effective teachers have: being highly effective was not positively associated with higher levels of qualifications in mathematics. What did predict effectiveness was the amount of continuing professional development in mathematics education a teacher had undertaken.

The key thing that distinguished highly effective teachers from the others was a consistent and coherent set of beliefs about how best to teach mathematics that took into account children's learning. We dubbed such a set of beliefs as having a *connectionist orientation* to teaching and learning. This connectionist orientation encompassed two things in particular:

- making connections within mathematics, both between different aspects of mathematics, for example, addition and subtraction or fractions, decimals and percentages, and between different representations of mathematics – symbols, words, diagrams and objects;
- making connections with children's methods – valuing these and being interested in children's thinking but also sharing other methods.

Improvisation and activity

Since this research into effective teachers I have been thinking about the metaphors we use in talking about teaching. What metaphors capture what these 'connectionist' teachers do? Trains and gardens are both too far removed from involving a collective of people. Some find the metaphor of an orchestra helpful, with teacher as the conductor, but that has too many overtones for me of the teacher/conductor as the 'sage on the stage'. A metaphor for thinking about teaching that I do find both appealing and helpful is from theatre and improvisational drama in particular. To act like the 'connectionist' teachers and take account of the learners' contribution as well as the mathematics, a certain amount of improvisation is needed in lessons. What happens in mathematics lessons is, in a sense, a performance that unfolds as the lesson develops.

Performance in some of the educational literature has pejorative overtones. For example, Dweck (2000) talks of 'performance oriented' learners as learners who are keen to be seen to 'perform' in correct and acceptable ways but that such 'performances' might not be linked to understandings. Similarly there are overtones sometimes of being taught to 'perform' in the 'training' sense of the word.

In contrast to such views of performance as not being creative or allowing for agency, I am using the term as used by Lois Holzman, in that the majority of our daily activity could be thought of as having an element of performance, and an unscripted one at that: any good conversation has an element of improvised performance. Holzman argues that one reading of Vygotsky is that we learn and develop through performing.

> Performative psychology is based in an understanding of human life as primarily performative, that is, we collectively create our lives through performing (simultaneously being who we are and who we are becoming).
>
> (Holzman 2000: 88)

Looking back I think that our 'connectionist teachers' were skilled at 'collectively creating' their mathematics lessons by including the children's performances in that collectivity. This is not typical of all mathematics lessons. Although very young children learn to talk through joining in performances of conversations that are co-created and improvised between the child and more experienced others, as they grow older much of what children learn, particularly in mathematics lessons, becomes 'routinized and rigidified into behavior' (Holzman ibid.). An important distinction that Holzman makes here is between behavior and activity: the former being a focus on the 'self-contained individual' and activity as what people engage in together 'rather than as the external manifestation of an individualized, internal process', much as I have been distinguishing action and activity.

One activity that some adults engage in which is performative in the sense of collectively creative is improvisational drama, in which actors create scenes without a pre-determined script. Mathematical problem solving could be considered similar to improvisational drama. Of course much of what passes for problem solving in school mathematics would be better described as exercises in that the method of solution is, in a sense, scripted (pre-determined, pre-scripted) and all the performer (child) has to do is replace certain elements. But problems for which pupils do not have a 'script' can be understood as improvisational. Improvisational drama (improv) provides a metaphorical lens for examining problem-solving activity and helps us to think about assumptions and practices.

Improvisational drama

From the outside, improvisational drama may look like it is all freedom and no discipline. On the contrary, it only works if the 'players' are highly disciplined. Let me illustrate this through a hypothetical example based on taking part in some training in this and the challenges it presented. In the language of improv, scenes unfold through a series of 'offerings' – the discipline lies in how the participants pick up and play with the offerings. So, a scene may start with an offering from the audience as to the location of the action. 'Garden' a voice calls out from the dark.

> I kneel down and start planting carrots.
> Carrie walks in.
> 'Oh no, what happened to Fido?'

This is a typical start to an improv scene. Someone suggests a location, and you start to mime some action linked to that. The scene develops through 'players' (often only two) making offerings: my initial offering is to be digging something and Carrie accepts this and her offering is to suggest that I am burying a dog. A key rule in the discipline is 'Yes and' – to make the scene work, to make it build, the trick is to take Carrie's offering and build on it.

> 'I'm sorry, I was hoping to get him buried before you got home.'

On paper, this sounds like the easiest thing in the world to do. In practice it's damn difficult. More often what comes out is something like:

> 'What do you mean? Can't you see that I'm planting carrots?'

What came home forcibly to me through such experiences is the difficulty of getting out of your own way. If I have decided this scene is going to be about growing vegetables, then that is what it is going to be about. It is hard to give up the need to be in control. Who knows where the scene might go if we head off in a different direction? But letting go, trusting that between you something worthwhile will emerge is what you have to do. And when you do, something richer and more interesting usually emerges. Relinquishing some control as the teacher has, I find, similar benefits.

Whose maths is it anyway?

I am suggesting that mathematics classrooms could unfold in ways that bear some resemblance to the way that improv scenes unfold, and that, when we trust to that process, the maths that emerges is more interesting and pupils are more engaged. Why do I see such similarities? I suggest teachers are frequently presented with 'offerings' to which they have to respond.

For example, a Reception class I visited was working on 'sorting'. One group of children had been given paper with two circles drawn on it and a collection of plastic bears in different sizes to sort into the two circles. Josh had put some yellow and blue bears into the circles and the teacher had taken a photograph of this to display on the whiteboard and talk about with the class. Josh's picture looked something like Figure 4.1.

The class discussion of the photograph began:

> Teacher: Josh, tell the class how you sorted the bears.
> Josh: Into big and little.
> Teacher: I think Josh has forgotten how he sorted the bears. Can anyone help him?

Figure 4.1 Josh's sorting of the bears

Josh was invited to provide an offering to the class, but the teacher negated Josh's offering. Chatting to her afterwards, from her point of view this was perfectly reasonable. She had an agenda of sorting into the two circles and the possibility of straying into talking about the sorting in a different way, reading across the rows – large bears at the top and small bears underneath – was not a direction she wanted to go in at that time. But this is the equivalent of my insisting that the scene I am in has to be about planting vegetables. In fact in the lesson I did suggest we might ask Josh why he said large and small and he clearly could articulate how there were two big bears across the top and two smaller ones across the bottom. The class were able to talk about how Josh's way of laying out the bears could be read in two different ways – looking across at the sizes and down at the colors. I am not suggesting that these five-year-olds then all went off to sort in two directions, but a seed of mathematics was planted, that, for some, moved the activity on from a simple sorting into two groups.

This may sound critical of the teacher but it is not meant to be. My experience of improv brought home how this is such a common way of reacting. After all the time we put into planning lessons and the imperative to specify in advance what the learning outcome is going to be, then we need to keep it 'on track'. There's the track metaphor again, but keeping it on track assumes the track is the only route. And like the 'gardening story' the scene that unfolds could be less or more interesting.

Many researchers have documented the common pattern in classroom interactions of 'initiation-response-feedback' (IRF) (Sinclair and Coulthard 1975). The teacher initiates a response from a child or the class (How did you sort your bears?). A child responds (into big or little). The teacher provides feedback on the response (I think you have forgotten). Children quickly learn from IRF interactions that the teacher is the judge of whether or not what they say is acceptable. This has two knock-on effects. First, the conversation easily turns into 'guess what's in the teacher's head'. Children do not offer what they really think; they offer what they think the teacher wants to hear. Second, the discussion gets closed down as children who are not confident that their offering is 'correct' (in the ears of the teacher) become reluctant to risk something that is possibly not acceptable.

Downward causation

Complexity theorists talk about the phenomena of downward causation (Campbell 1974). 'In downward causation, an emergent higher level property begins to cause effects in the lower level, either in the agents or in their patterns of interaction' (Sawyer 1999: 455). Although it is not our usual way of thinking and talking about learning, the evidence does point to it making sense to talk of downward causation in the sense of the mathematics that children collectively produce having an effect back on the learners. Josh's sorting of the bears was, whether or not he intended it to be, a higher level of mathematics than the teacher had planned or expected. Picking up on this allowed for conversation that opened up the possibility of downward causation.

Experienced improvisers testify to downward causation. At the beginning of a scene, improvising actors have a whole range of options open to them (indeed, one of the disciplines of improv is to keep these options open for as long as possible), but once the form and content of the scene starts to emerge, actors will talk afterwards of the scene 'writing itself'. Similarly jazz musicians report a sense of the music playing the band:

> The players thus develop a collective direction that characteristically – as though the participants had all read Emile Durkheim – feels larger than any of them, as though it had a life of its own. It feels as though, instead of them playing the music, the music, Zen-like, is playing them.
>
> (Becker 2000: 172)

As children improvise solutions to mathematical problems, the (tacit) sense of the solutions having some agency rather than being the 'property' of specific children may account for why I find that even at a young age children are able to talk about the solutions without being defensive or possessive of them. Even if it is only metaphorical to talk of downward causation, engendering a sense of this plays, I suggest, an important role in moving from either a teacher-centered or a pupil-centered lesson to a mathematics-centered one.

> Likewise, people must have a real shared interest in getting the job done, an interest powerful enough to overcome divisive selfish interests. In an improvising musical or theatrical group, for instance, no one must be interested in making a reputation or protecting one already made.
>
> (Becker 2000: 175)

Summary

Allowing an element of improvisation to come into play in mathematics, particularly through working on unstructured problems, is a way of engaging children in mathematical activity rather than simply doing actions.

Further reading

Engaging Minds: Learning and Teaching in a Complex World, by Brent Davis, Dennis Sumara and Rebecca Luce-Kaplar. This is a great introduction to complexity theory and the implications for teaching.

Metaphors We Live By, by George Lakoff and Mark Johnson. A slim but powerful book that will change the way you think about language and challenge the idea that we can simply 'put' ideas 'into' words.

Part 2

Transforming primary mathematics

Chapter 5

Mathematical activity
Mindful or fluent?

> The capacity to achieve an outcome is different from the ability to explore the
> world and understand experience. Trying to solve a math problem in a way dictated
> by the teacher is different from attempting to test one's own hypothesis. The
> teacher who tells students to solve a problem in a prescribed manner is limiting
> their ability to investigate their surroundings and to test novel ideas.
>
> (Langer 1997)

In previous chapters I have argued for changes in how we think about primary mathematics learning, curriculum and teaching. I questioned the positioning of the individual
learner at the center of teaching and argued that we need to shift our attention from
thinking about the *actions* that children might engage in during mathematics lessons to
looking more holistically at the totality of *activity* which learning mathematics is located
within. Alongside this we need to look at our expectations for collective activity in the
classroom and achieve a balance between attending to the individuals in a class and the
classroom collective and accept that having goals for the collective are as important as
having them for the individuals.

Turning attention to the curriculum I examined how the emphasis on describing the
curriculum as a body of content, as knowledge, comes with its attendant metaphor of
packages, of commodities to be delivered in small pieces. With the uncertainty of what
mathematics learners will need for the future we need to pay more attention to the
process of coming to know rather than the end results.

With regard to teaching I argued that the metaphor of performance rather than
preformed might be helpful in moving our attention. Successful performance depends
on engaging in co-constructing emergent mathematical activity.

In this chapter I look in more detail at learning outcomes in primary mathematics
and suggest that these are essentially of two different sorts: mindful learning and fluency.
I argue that these different sorts of outcomes require different pedagogies and we need
to be careful not to confuse these.

Mathematical activity

My starting point for thinking about mathematical activity comes from Cuoco,
Goldenberg, and Mark's idea of 'habits of mind' that include:

learning to recognize when problems or statements that purport to be mathematical are, in truth, still quite ill-posed or fuzzy; becoming comfortable with and skilled at bringing mathematical meaning to problems and statements through definition, systematization, abstraction, or logical connection making; and seeking and developing new ways of describing situations. Although it is necessary to infuse courses and curricula with modern content, what is even more important is to give students the tools they will need in order to use, understand, and even make mathematics that does not yet exist.

A curriculum organized around habits of mind tries to close the gap between what the users and makers of mathematics do and what they say. Such a curriculum lets students in on the process of creating, inventing, conjecturing, and experimenting; it lets them experience what goes on behind the study door before new results are polished and presented.

(Cuoco, Goldenberg *et al.* 1996: 376)

While I find some appeal in the notion of habit as it moves us towards the idea that mathematics is learnable rather than innate, the phrase 'habits of mind' still, for me, has too many overtones of the centrality of the individual (and the 'work' of doing mathematics being an internal, private affair). All of the things that Cuoco and colleagues suggest people do are also collective activities: mathematicians jointly create conjectures through talking about patterns, sharing methods and discussing strategies. Indeed it is the collective activity that drives much of this. There is little point in describing or conjecturing for its own sake. It is through being immersed in such group activities that individuals come to take on board such habits of mind.

But isn't all this beyond what primary school children can do? Isn't this the formal, abstract activity of mathematics that (some) children can engage in once they have learnt 'the basics'? Such questions implicitly fall back on (Piagetian) ideas of qualitatively different stages and levels of thinking. Cognitive scientists now argue that there is little evidence of a thinking stages theory of development and that young children can think in as many different ways as adults (Goswami and Bryant 2010). Any apparent differences are more likely to be down to lack of experience and the fact that children (and adults) need multisensory experiences. It is the schooling approach of presenting the mathematical activities listed above in only one form – abstract symbolic – that prevents younger children from engaging in these activities, not the nature of the thinking itself. Take, for example, the belief that young children cannot 'deal' with a calculation such as $3 \div 4$. As Terezhina Nunes pointed out in a talk of hers, show me a group of four children who would turn away an offer of three bars of chocolate on the basis of 'you cannot divide three by four'. So my starting point is to take activities out of which habits of mind might emerge, rather than going immediately to the cognitive, to the individual. The practices are much more the result of induction into mathematical activity (Bruner 1986) than individual mental activity.

The power of being inducted into mathematical activity and how 'invisible' this can be, in the sense of what you come to take for granted, came home forcefully for me in a professional development session I once led. I had given out scientific calculators for the teachers to work with and one of them called me over.

'My 5 quid calculator has got a $\frac{1}{x}$ button on, so why doesn't this expensive one?'
'Well, it does', I replied, 'it's that x^{-1} button.'

This seemed an opportunity to explore powers and so I stopped everyone to go through the argument as to why, for consistency, mathematicians had decided to define x^{-1} as $\frac{1}{x}$. The teachers' nods during my explanation suggested that they were following me in the logic, but afterwards there was quite a lot of muttering going on at table of the teacher who had first called me over.

'Is there anything you are not clear about?' I enquired.
'No, we follow your argument,' the teacher replied. 'But we were just saying to each other, "why would anyone ever want to do that in the first place?"'

Why indeed? I don't think that I was born with a gene that developed into this habit of mind. I did do a mathematics degree and while much of the 'hard' content of what I had been taught I can no longer remember, I had been successfully inducted into the mathematical activity of pushing the boundaries of definitions and generalities. That was not something I'd ever been explicitly taught; it was a tacit understanding that had come about through being with groups of people – experienced mathematicians and novices – where that was the activity that you engaged in. In this chapter I explore how we might involve primary children in similar activity, starting by thinking about reasoning as collaborative mathematical activity rather than being in individuals' heads.

Reasoning as activity

'A fool with a tool is still a fool.'

I don't know where this quote originally comes from, but it sums up why I think reasoning is so central to learning about mathematics. The literature is replete with studies telling of how children can learn the 'tools' of mathematics – methods of long multiplication, how to find the answer to a division calculation – yet still not be able to use or apply these tools outside the context of worksheets or the classroom. In these circumstances it is easy to fall back on thinking that children are the 'fools' – that they would be able to use the mathematical tools that they have been taught, if only they were brighter, less distracted, worked harder or any other of a multitude of reasons.

We tend to think of reasoning as something that is both private and internal and often an extended process, as in reasoning through the solution to a difficult problem. I want to look at reasoning as also a micro-activity, something that we actually draw upon a lot in learning mathematics, but which becomes hidden to us when ideas are very familiar. For example we often use the language of 'recognize' in describing mathematical learning: children learn to recognize what a half is, or to recognize that Figure 5.1 is a cube (see Figure 5.1).

Of course, it is not a cube at all, but a hexagon. In 'recognizing' this as a cube I have to set aside all sorts of things that I know about cubes, such as the fact that they have square faces: only one of the quadrilaterals in Figure 5.1 is square. Children have difficulty setting aside what they know and so early representations of cubes look like Figure 5.2.

If mathematical ideas are thought of as transparently self-evident, then to recognize in the sense of 'identify as already known' (Oxford English Dictionary) is appropriate.

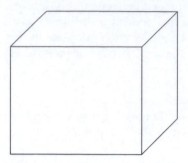

Figure 5.1 Is this a cube?

Figure 5.2 A child's drawing of a cube

But another definition of recognize is 'realize or discover the nature of'. It is this second sense that I want to explore through some examples in the context of fractions.

Recognize this?

Before reading on, take a look at Figure 5.3 and decide what fraction you think the shaded part represents (adapted from Lamon 2005).

If I now tell you that the unshaded part could represent 3⅔, does that make you question your interpretation of the shaded part? People's initial reaction to this diagram is usually to interpret it as representing 2¾. So 'natural' does this interpretation appear, that it almost doesn't seem possible that it could be 3⅔. Yet it can and I invite you to spend a moment or two thinking about how this diagram can be interpreted in a way that means the unshaded part sensibly represents 3⅔. What does that then make the shaded part?

Consider 3⅔ as its equivalent in thirds – ¹¹⁄₃. There are 12 small squares in the diagram and 11 of them are unshaded. Each small square could then represent one third. So if we take our 'unit' as three squares, then the shaded part can indeed represent 3⅔.

Figure 5.3 What fraction is the unshaded part?

I am not cheating here. There is no mathematical rule that says 'units' (three squares as a unit in this particular case) must always be presented unambiguously. There are many ways that $1\frac{1}{3}$ can be laid out. The trouble is that we are used to images where the unit is assumed to be spelt out by the way the diagram is presented, rather than having to reason through what the unit is. Before reading on, you might like to consider some of the other fractions that a single small square in the diagram could represent. Could it be $\frac{1}{2}$? Could it be $\frac{1}{12}$? Could it be $\frac{1}{6}$? School experiences of fractions present them in ways that reduce ambiguity. I am arguing, for reasons that I will spell out shortly, that ambiguity, or 'conditionality' as Langer calls it (it could be $\frac{1}{4}$ or it could be $\frac{1}{3}$, it all depends), is likely to improve learning rather than lead to confusion.

A key question arises in the context of this fraction example – exactly where does the one third exist? Or the $\frac{1}{4}$ exist? Or any of the other possible fractions that the unshaded square can be interpreted as? If mathematics exists 'out there' as suggested by discovery or perception metaphors (see Chapter 4), then the 'knowledge' of shaded-as-one-third (or whatever) must precede anybody's engagement with the diagram. As I hope you have just appreciated, there are many possible interpretations of the value of the unshaded square. There is no 'absolute' fractional value embedded within the white square; it depends on the perspective that the knower brings to it. The 'usual' interpretation of $\frac{1}{4}$ has been socially agreed upon (by the community of mathematicians) as being the one that everyone might best adhere to. Any 'knowledge' of the value of the shaded square cannot be separated from the 'knower', or from the community (mathematical or classroom) that has agreed on the most appropriate or useful interpretation. Coming to know about fractions, or any other aspect of mathematics, cannot be separated from the network of mathematical activity that gave rise to fractions in the first place *and* the network of activities within which learning about fractions is embedded. The better aligned these are, the more 'knowing' will come about. Problem solving is what aligns these two networks of activity. Engaging with others in questioning and exploring the activities of working with fractions can help learners 'realize or discover the nature of' fractions as being a human construction, arising from and being used in activity, rather than being 'objects' that have some sort of existence outside this activity.

If you think this is all a bit esoteric and beyond the realm of primary mathematics, then consider the example in Figure 5.4 similar to one from England's 2008 national test for 11-year-olds. I expect that the answer to the question being $\frac{1}{5}$ and not $\frac{2}{5}$ would fox as many adults as children.

Mindful learning

Although I have been arguing for moving away from overly focusing on the individual in mathematics learning and teaching, that does not mean that I am not also interested in the learning of individual pupils. It is the limitations of an emphasis on the individual and only seeing the collective as being of service to the individuals that needs balancing in the view of attending to the collective and the individuals co-constructing it. Nevertheless, as noted by Lois Holzman, individuals are distinguishable from the collective if not separable. It is still legitimate to look at the individual.

Rather than talk of the individual's learning in terms of understanding, I am drawn toward considering most of mathematics learning to be linked to what Ellen Langer describes as 'mindful' learning (Langer 1997). Mindful is a term redolent with overtones

One third of this square is shaded

The same square is used in the diagram below.
What fraction of this new diagram is shaded?

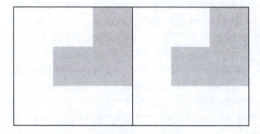

Figure 5.4 What fraction?

of Zen and meditation but Langer uses it to mean learning with awareness and of being 'mindful' of the nature of the knowledge in the sense of not simply taking it as unquestioned givens. A key element of being mindful, Langer argues, is an awareness of the conditionality of much knowledge. Treating knowledge as 'conditional' – that it holds under certain conditions – makes for more powerful learning experiences. For example, in one of Langer's experiments she presented two groups of high school students' images of ambiguous pictures.

> We presented the pictures either conditionally ('This could be . . .') or with absolute language ('This is . . .') and asked the students to remember them. Tests of recall and recognition of the objects in a new context revealed that conditional learning resulted in better memory.
>
> (Langer 1997: 80)

Even if you still think children only need to be taught to 'recognize' fractions, then Langer's research suggests that they should at least be introduced conditionally.

Ah yes, I hear, but mathematics is not conditional, it is absolute. Children have to know that 2 + 2 = 4 and not think that it could be 5 or a banana. Well, yes and no. Some simple arithmetical facts are not that 'open' to being conditional, but even then most mathematics is not that fixed. Pour two glasses of water into a jug, followed by another two and you don't end up with four glasses of water. More seriously, a lack of conditionality when it comes to different calculations can make a difference. For example, typically, children meet multiplication predominantly as repeated addition. So, four bags of five apples can be represented by 4 × 5. But so can:

- A tray of cakes 4 by 5 (multiplication could be an array)
- The area of a rectangle 4 cm by 5 cm (multiplication could be an area)
- The height of a beanstalk that was 4 m tall and has grown to be five times as tall (multiplication could be scaling)
- The number of sprats that a mother whale eats if she eats 5 sprats for every one her baby eats and the baby eats 4 (multiplication could be ratio)
- The number of wheels on five cars (multiplication could be rate).

Four times five could be five added four times but it could also be lots of other things. Four groups of five is a conditional interpretation, but children come to regard this as absolute. Just as Langer's students became limited in their views when told 'this is a (balloon, or whatever)' so children become limited in their views of multiplication when told 'this is repeated addition'. Then when presented with, say, ½ × ¾ they get stuck because their thinking goes along the lines of 'How is this addition? How can I add a half three-quarter times?' rather than ask themselves what else the multiplication could be. An area perhaps?

To take another example, 12 ÷ 4 could be the mathematical model for at least two different things: the result of sharing out 12 objects equally between 4 people (division as sharing or partitioning) or the result of putting 12 objects into bags of 4 (division as repeated subtraction or quotitioning). Division as sharing tends to be the model most frequently focused on. Julia Anghileri (2001) has a lovely example of the limiting power of a lack of awareness of the conditionality of division as sharing. Two eleven-year-old girls are trying to figure out what 12 ÷ ½ could be. They used only the language of 'sharing' to try and make sense of the calculation and repeatedly ask themselves 'what can she (the teacher) mean? How can you share between a half?' Eventually they decide that the fraction must be wrong and what they are really being asked to do is 12 ÷ 2, ending up with 6 as the answer. Not being mindful of different possibilities the girls end up making the 'reality' (that is the question on the page) fit their (only) interpretation, rather than consider other conditions in which this might be possible to interpret in a meaningful fashion.

Cathy Fosnot and her colleagues have some other examples of working with conditionality from her 'Young Mathematicians at Work' project. In one of the detailed case-study lessons, the teacher introduces her class of eight- and nine-year-olds to both models of division – partitioning and quotitioning – through the context of looking at the numbers of drinks cans required to fill two dispensing machines. The teacher explains to the class how one of the machines in the staffroom holds only cans of coke. As she was sitting there one day, the guy arrived to stock up the machine and told her that it held 126 cans. That got her wondering how many 'six-packs' that would mean bringing home from the supermarket. The children are not sent off to immediately work on this problem, but the teacher goes on to tell of how she found out that the second machine holds six different flavors of drink and also 126 cans in total. Her question about that machine is that if there are the same number of cans of each flavor, how many is that? (See Cameron, Dolk *et al.* 2005 for full details, including videos of the lesson.)

It is easy to think that both these problems are 'just' 126 ÷ 6. Indeed to most adults they present little difficulty. But the children are only just learning about division: many of them use quite different strategies to solve each problem and initially do not see how they might both be modeled by the same division calculation. The materials around this case study show how skillfully the teacher discusses with the class the links and how 126 ÷ 6 can be used to model each situation. By ending up with the one mathematical model for the two different problems, the conditional nature of what a division calculation might represent is foregrounded.

This is a markedly different approach to introducing the children to one model of division (usually 'sharing') and thinking that they need to 'get to grips' with that model before 'confusing' them with a different model. The difficulty in that approach is that, whichever model is introduced first, the children are likely to accept that as 'the' model, rather than a conditional model. To take another case, many of us still always read a subtraction calculation as 'take-away' when treating it as finding the difference may be more sensible, I suspect as a result of the early introduction of 'take-away' prior to finding differences.

A key thing here is whether our focus is on finding answers to calculations or becoming mindful of the underlying mathematics. We still devote too much time to the former, when we have calculators that can now do that for us. It is imaginable, although unlikely, that a calculator or computer could one day be 'mindful', but for the moment this is a uniquely human trait that we need to nurture. Developing a mindful approach to mathematics can start early, as the case study of Socks and Sticks shows.

Socks and sticks

We presented a class of five-year-olds with two problems. For the first, I had taken in a bag of 12 socks. Emptying the socks on the floor, two children volunteered to count them and we all agreed that there were 12. My question was, when my socks were put back together in pairs, how many pairs of socks would that be?

Before setting the children off to figure out the answer to my sock problem, I posed a second.

We talked about Chinese meals and whether any of the children had ever used chopsticks. Some pairs of chopsticks were passed around for people to try out. The problem was this: six friends went out for a Chinese meal together. How many chopsticks would they need for them to have a pair each?

Could any of the children be mindful of a link here and realize that, mathematically, there was a connection between six pairs of socks and six pairs of chopsticks? Could they become mindful that the mathematical expression of 6 + 6 could be used to model both situations?

Most of the children, as we expected, were not immediately mindful of any link. After all, socks are socks and chopsticks are chopsticks. Joe's work (Figure 5.5) is typical of the children's first attempts. He found a solution to one problem, found a solution to the second, but did not see any connection between the two.

continued . . .

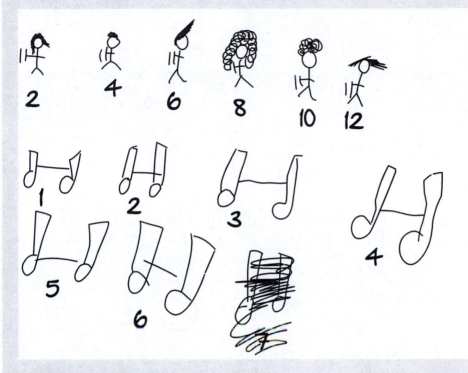

Figure 5.5 Joe's solution

Dylan initially started off like Joe, but having found his two solutions and that both contexts involved six pairs, he realized that there must be some connection. So he drew out again the six pairs of chopsticks, mirroring the way he had set out six pairs of socks. This marks a key step on the way to a mindful generalization: the patterning of the layout of the socks in exactly the same way as the layout of the chopsticks strongly suggests that Joe is paying less attention to whether the items in the problem are socks or chopsticks and more attention to how these can be modeled mathematically in similar ways. Such shifts of attention are central to mathematical activity: I discuss them further below when I look at variation theory in the next chapter.

Meg was the only child to instantly claim that there was a connection between the two problems. She announced that they were the same and so we asked her what she meant by that and if she could put something down on paper to convince us why she claimed this. She started off by showing us that six people holding a chopstick in each hand were matched by giving a pair of socks to each person. She then wrote a little mathematical proof as shown by the two equations in her bubble (Figure 5.7). We noted that she was recording 12 as 21 but judged this as something that we would need to sort out later rather than correct it within the course of this

continued . . .

Figure 5.6 Dylan's solution

lesson, as that might have diverted Meg's attention from sharing her reasoning with us and set up the alternative expectation that what we were really interested in was 'correct' recordings. Drawing a sock and recording that there were 12 of these above her first equation, and then a chopstick and that there were 12 of these above her second equation, she drew an arrow linking the first equation to the second and another arrow in the reverse direction. As she explained 'This [pointing to the sock equation] is the same as this [the chopstick equation] because six pairs of socks is 12 and six pairs of chopsticks is 12, and this [chopstick equation] is the same as this [the sock equation] and it goes round like that forever.'

The lesson was drawn together with Dylan and Meg sharing their methods. While not claiming that all the children had by then come to be mindful of the mathematical link between the two problems, it was clear that everyone in the class was moving forward in their thinking.

continued . . .

Figure 5.7 Meg's solution

Meg is already demonstrating the mathematical activity of looking to the connections – by getting her to come to the front and explain why she thought the two problems were the same we were able to begin to raise other children's awareness of the need to look for connections.

Fluency

While much more of mathematics learning needs to be mindful, I am wary of arguing this for all mathematics. There are some aspects that children need to be reasonably fluent in. Some things are best done fairly automatically. If you know that eight add two is ten, then the door is open to exploring some mathematics that involves adding numbers to ten. If, on the other hand, you need still to count in ones from eight to ten then your attention, your mindfulness, is going to be taken up with the counting and you could lose sight of what you were aiming for. However, much less of the mathematics curriculum needs to be at the level of fluency than we currently aim for.

Research by Jenny Young-Loveridge and her colleagues nicely demonstrates the impact of such demands on your attention with some research done with young children (Young-Loveridge, Carr *et al.* 1995). They assessed four-year-olds on a number of mathematical tasks, one of which was 'give me five'. If you put out five objects and ask a young child to count them, many will be able to do so, but it is much more difficult for young children to give you five objects from a larger collection. Some children at the age of four were able to count out five (and being able to do this was a good predictor of these children's mathematical attainment at age 11); others were 'grabbers' who would simply scoop up a handful of items without counting them. The children of interest here were those who could count out from the collection but not stop when they had reached five: the actions of counting out and holding on to the need to stop at five are too much to coordinate and hold together in short-term memory.

I have tried this with many children, stopping them after they have gone a few beyond five, replacing them all and reminding them that I only want five. At about the third time round this children start to watch your face – they know that a glimmer of a smile or a slightly raised eyebrow will signal to them when to stop. I like to think that this is an indication of the social, distributed brain – how we use others around us to take some of the cognitive load. Stanislas Dehaene in his wonderful book *The Number Sense* (1999) tells the story of a famous counting horse in France around the turn of the twentieth century. Scientists finally figured out that the horse's trainer was very subtly signaling to the horse when to stop counting. Somewhat sadly the trainer himself was surprised he had been doing this – he wasn't aware of his signaling this and was disappointed to learn of the horse's lack of arithmetical ability.

Learning the tables still seems to be one of those 'hot potatoes' or touchstones in mathematics education. Your answer to 'do children need to learn their tables?' is a marker of whether or not you are a 'progressive educator' or a believer in 'back to basics'. Both of these miss the point of being fluent in addition and multiplication bonds. They treat knowing these as an end in themselves. But the point of being fluent in them is to free up the working memory when tackling a more interesting and engaging piece of mathematics. It's like learning to touch-type. Years ago I was a reasonably quick two-finger typist, but I had to watch my fingers as I typed and I had to work from handwritten notes outlining what I was going to write about before I could type it up. I couldn't think about the content and type at the same time – too much of my available mental attention was taken up with the latter to be able to process the former simultaneously. But work with a highly behaviorist drill and practice teach-yourself-to-touch-type program moved me forward and I can now (and am as I write this chapter) think and produce the content as I type – my typing is fluent enough for the part of my brain that deals with this to get on with it without my needing to bring conscious attention to it.

The case study 'Jellybeans' (see Chapter 2) illustrates the importance of fluency. As a challenge for six- and seven-year-olds this is a difficult problem. Had they only been confident in counting on in ones then figuring out the answer would have got in the way of actually thinking about different ways of getting there. So two things were firmly in place before we posed the problem to the children. The first was being fluent in adding 10 to any number up to 1000. This expectation is actually beyond what is in the curriculum but if you can add 10 to any number up to 100 then you can actually add 10 to any number! We could have gone beyond 1000 but then there is the additional burden on the short-term memory of simply 'holding' the number that 10 is being added to: 'six thousand seven hundred and forty six' takes up six chunks of short-term memory and as an adult generally can only work with seven or so items in short-term memory, then expecting a six-year-old to hold onto the number and add ten to it is setting them up to fail. But 'seven hundred and forty six add 10' is just about manageable. This was a fluency skill that we worked on little and often and we made our expectations clear to the children. They weren't simply told that they were 'learning to add ten'; we modeled the rapidity with which we were expecting this to be done. Working on this fluency started off with children firing numbers at the teacher who rapidly responded with the number ten more, making it explicit that there was an expectation of being able to fire back the answer without much of a pause. Over the course of the first term we worked on this in frequent short bursts. It's difficult to describe in words the style of doing this, but a number would be called out and a child pointed at. If they didn't rapidly call out the number ten more then they were told 'too late' and the same number directed to other children until one did respond quickly and correctly. Lest this sounds like the old style of testing tables that left some people with a life-long dread of mathematics through the public shame of not getting it right, the whole thing was done in a light-hearted playful manner where lots of people (including the adults in the room) were 'too late' so that no one was being singled out. Even once the answer was got, the same number might be repeated, back to some of the children who had previously not got it in time so that everyone ended up being successful. Whenever we asked the class if they wanted to play the 'add ten' challenge they enthusiastically agreed. And over time, repeatedly hearing and joining in on 'sixty-seven, seventy-six, forty-five, fifty-five' embedded the knowing that adding ten leaves the unit unchanged.

Elements of fluency

In moving up through the years of primary mathematics children are hampered if they are not fluent in:

- adding or subtracting a single digit to any number;
- adding a multiple of 10 or 100 to any number;
- counting on or back in ones from any starting number;
- counting on or back in twos, tens, or fives from any starting number;
- recalling rapidly the multiplication facts up to 10×10;
- multiplying any number by 2 or 10.

It is crucial that we are clear and explicit about what the activity of being fluent involves. In one school I worked with, the teachers of seven-year-olds were discussing with the teachers of the year below what they hoped the children might be fluent in when they moved up a year. Fluency in knowing the pairs of numbers that add to ten was a generally agreed desirable. The teachers of the younger age group claimed that this was something that most children left their classes able to do. Exploring this further it became clear that their meaning of fluency was being able to answer, say, 6 + 4, by any method, whereas the teachers in the year above were hoping for this to be a known fact. We need to make sure that common language does not mean an assumption of common activity. And we need to ensure that children are not simply left to their own devices in becoming fluent – that this develops 'naturally'. One of our research projects demonstrated the power of actively working on developing children's fluency.

In the 'Raising attainment in numeracy project' (Askew, Bibby *et al.* 1997) my colleagues Tamara Bibby and Margaret Brown and I worked with seven-year-olds who were deemed to be behind their peers in the level of mathematics that they were engaging in. Together with a group of teacher researchers we developed a program of 15 minutes intensive one-to-one intervention that the children were engaged in once a week for several weeks. One of our conjectures was that it was the children's lack of fluency in simple calculating strategies that was hampering their progress. We based the focus of the intervention work on research that suggested that there were distinct stages that children went through in becoming fluent. So, for example, in becoming fluent in knowing that 6 + 5 = 11, children might:

- Count all: The child might need to model physical objects, such as counters or fingers, to find the answer to the question by putting out six objects and then five and then counting the total.
- Count on: Here the child can hold 'six' in their head and count on the additional five, usually by holding up extra fingers one at a time.
- Derived fact: Here the child can use a fact that they are already fluent in to figure out the answer to one they do not know. Knowing 5 + 5 = 10, the child can figure out that 6 + 5 must be one more.
- Known fact: When a pupil answers too rapidly to have used a calculating strategy and indicates that she or he simply knows the answer.

Notice that being fluent in what appear to be quite basic skills requires some connections between these. For example, a child who is not confident in counting on in ones from any number cannot appropriate the technique of counting on. So we also got the children to practice counting on and back in various steps.

The children in our program were assessed one-on-one on a diagnostic interview before and after the intervention (Denvir and Bibby 1997). We had a matched sample of children in a control group who were also individually assessed at the same time as the children in the program. The progress of the target children was statistically significantly greater than that of the control group in terms of improvement in the number of things they got correct on the assessment after the intervention. As well as this quantitative difference in what the children could do, there was a qualitative difference in how they were answering the questions.

We were able to identify these qualitative differences because the assessment interviews allowed us to code the strategies that the children had used on each occasion, not simply whether they got the answer right. Where children in the control group demonstrated growth in the strategies that they used, their improvements closely corresponded to the order of the stages outlined above. The children in the intervention group, however, showed greater progress in the strategies they used. For example, many who had used a 'modeling' strategy in the first interview used derived and known facts on the second interview. We don't know whether they had 'skipped' over counting on or moved rapidly through that stage, but our findings showed clearly that as teachers we do not simply have to wait until children adopt more efficient strategies. That carefully targeted intervention can speed things up.

We had set out to develop an intervention that we could show *did* work, rather than gather evidence on *why* it worked, but our observations and audio-recordings of many of the intervention sessions provided us with some insights into what made the difference. The first thing that we noticed was that often teachers had assumed that pupils demonstrating success on a particular aspect of fluency suggested full mastery of the skill. For example, many children were initially judged to be fluent in counting on in twos. Indeed, they presented themselves as such. Asked to count in twos they would confidently start 'two, four, six, eight . . .' Around about reaching 'thirty' teachers would often say, 'OK, thank you', but if not, then the child herself would stop, as though she had demonstrated enough not to need to go on. Rather than being satisfied with this, we got the teachers to ask the children to 'carry on': in many cases counting in 2s to 30 was the limit of the child's performance. As a result of this, one of the activities that we introduced into each intervention session was to work on counting, starting the activity at a large, unusual number. 'Let's count in 2s and start at 76.' Watching the evident satisfaction of the children as they came to be mindful of the fact that counting on in 2s, or whatever, was a generalizable skill that they could apply to any starting number seemed to be one of the 'keys' to unlocking confidence and success.

Another aspect that became clear was that it seemed that children had not previously been made aware of what becoming fluent might actually look like. We got teachers to model this for the children by 'turning the tables' – children would give problems to the teacher who would demonstrate how quickly she could work these out. The children were impressed by how quickly the adults were able to do things and wanted to know the 'secret' of being able to do this. Because these children had, up until then, been heavily dependent on working practically – using counters or fingers – it appeared that many of them thought that mathematics was itself a practical activity. Getting them to attend to working mentally helped change both their views of what engaging in mathematical activity means, and of themselves as learners.

An important insight was that the joint activities that teachers and children engage in might have inadvertently held back the development of fluency. For example, teachers might put out a collection of objects and ask: 'How many are there?' and the child would count the collection. Moments later the teacher might ask again 'So how many were there?' and the child would count again. We talked to the teachers about what they thought was going on here and the general opinion was that this was evidence that the children either had short-term memory difficulties or that they did not appreciate conservation of number. We suggested that next time that happened, the teacher might stop the child before they completed their second count, asking 'do you need to count them again?' In the vast majority of cases the child replied 'No' and could say how many things there were. From an activity theory perspective, the joint activity here was one with the tacit rule: asking how many there are means you must always count them. Changing the rules of the activity changed the 'ability' of the child.

We were not able to observe our intervention children in the context of their normal mathematics lessons but their teachers report that, for the majority, they had noticed a marked change in attitude. Whereas prior to the intervention these children had usually 'held back' in mathematics lessons, as they became more fluent and confident so they became much more engaged and involved in mathematics lessons. Maths had gone from being a mystery and an activity that they were excluded from to one where they were included.

Readiness?

It used to be a popularly held view that 'readiness' was a key factor in learning: children could not learn something before they were 'ready' to, in the sense that they had to have reached a certain 'level' of development before a new skill could be incorporated into what they could do. In terms of physical skills, there is a certain logic to this: clearly you cannot learn to run before you can walk. The dominance of Piaget's stage theories of learning contributed to the discourse of 'readiness': children had to work through each stage of development before they were 'ready' to engage in the type of thinking required of the next stage.

Although we do not talk about 'readiness' in such explicit terms, there was a sense from the teachers involved in the 'Raising Attainment' project of a residual belief in readiness; that children were using simple counting strategies because they were not 'ready' to move onto more sophisticated strategies. Many classrooms that I visit seem still to have echoes of this: children are engaged in lots of practical activities and are left to wean themselves off these when they are 'ready' rather than teachers actively intervening to change the nature of the activity that the child is engaged in. Recent research challenges the notion of readiness.

As I mentioned earlier, Usha Goswami and Peter Bryant, long-time scholars of Piaget's work, argue that there is actually no evidence for a stages theory of learning: the thinking mechanisms that we draw on as adults are actually pretty much in place from when we are born. It is lack of experience that limits what children can do, not any qualitatively different type of thinking. The British system does however seem wedded to a belief in stages (Goswami 2001). This supports my contention that we need to attend to the joint activities that we are engaged in with children much less than what they can or cannot do.

Work by Robert Siegler and Geetha Ramani (2009) with low-attaining children from low socio-economic backgrounds shows the power of working on activities rather than attributions. They worked on playing simple number track games and quickly the children were performing at a level comparable to their peers. Interestingly this research shows that to be effective the number tracks have to be linear rather than circular.

Comparative studies of education elsewhere also illustrate how the nature of the activities engaged in influences individual thinking. There is evidence that Chinese and Korean children are better at arithmetic than peers of the same age in America and that this is in part due to the use of more sophisticated strategies. For example, there is evidence that Asian children adopt addition strategies based on partitioning (decomposition) of digits rather than counting on in ones sooner than American peers. Calculating, say, 6 + 8, Korean children are more likely to decompose the 8 into 4 + 4 and calculate 6 + 4, and then 10 + 4 (Fuson and Kwon 1992), whereas American children of the same age would count on in ones. Research comparing Chinese and American children's strategies came to a similar conclusion: seven- and eight-year-old children in each nation differed in the 'back-up' strategies used for additions that they could not recall: Chinese children used this partitioning strategy earlier and more frequently, while U.S. children reverted to finger counting (Geary, Bow-Thomas *et al.* 1996). The hypothesis is that this is the result of the Asian language number naming system. In Korean and Chinese, 14 is named 'ten four' and this itself encourages the earlier and easier adoption of partitioning strategies: since children know 'ten' is an aspect of naming the final total they partition the numbers in order to make ten. Asian children are not innately 'brighter' mathematically, but the structuring of the activities that they engage in may make them appear so.

Procedural fluency

There are also a number of skills that I would dub 'semi-fluent', or procedural fluency as some dub it (National Research Council 2001) in the sense of knowing how to figure out the answer without a great deal of having to think through how to get there. Here I would include:

- knowing what to add to a number to make it up to a multiple of 10 or 100
- halving any number
- multiplying any number by 5 (by multiplying by 10 and halving)
- knowing the division facts associated with the multiplication facts.

Let me explain this last one: I have a conjecture that no one ever really does a mental division; knowing these is a result of being so secure in knowledge of multiplication facts. I have a strong sense that I know, say, that $36 \div 4$ is 9 because of the fluency in knowing that 9×4 is 36. So I think knowing the division facts is dependent on being really secure in multiplication facts.

But that is about it when it comes to mindless, or almost mindless, fluency. I think we are in danger when we see fluency as a goal of mathematics much beyond this limited set of arithmetical skills. This is a hard task, and many people will not agree; the measure of mathematical prowess for many is rapid and fluent ability in calculation. It may even catapult you from being a TV presenter to Government advisor. I don't think it will provide for most people the mathematical awareness that they need for their future lives.

Summary

I have suggested that there are two ways to approach mathematics: mindfully or mindlessly. Too much of current practice raises mindless learning over the mindful: for children to become successful young mathematicians we need to encourage them to adopt a much more mindful approach to mathematical activity. Becoming mindful is, however, supported by being fluent in certain skills.

We need to adopt different styles of pedagogy for these different learning outcomes. As much of current practice is directed toward fluency, in the next chapter I turn to looking at variation theory as a means to promote mindful learning.

Further reading

The Power of Mindful Learning by Ellen J. Langer. I hope you have gathered from this chapter that I am a big fan of this book. It is a slim volume and easily read in a single sitting but is packed with fascinating research and wise advice.

The Mindful Teacher by Elizabeth MacDonald and Dennis Shirley. Another slim but equally engaging and valuable volume. These authors are more focused on teachers' learning than pupils and draw on the Buddhist interpretations of mindfulness as well as Langer's work.

Chapter 6

Variation theory

During the past 120 years a great number of conceptualizations of learning have been promoted, all of them of course being researchers' conceptualizations. Exploring what learning means to the learner, how it is experienced, understood or conceptualized by her or him, is a comparatively recent, but dramatically expanding research specialization.

(Marton, Watkins *et al.* 1997)

In the previous chapter I argued that more of mathematics needs to be learnt as a mindful activity. The question then is how do we encourage children to be mindful? Rather like telling someone who is stuck to 'think' we cannot simply exhort children to be mindful. Part of the approach to this lies in fostering classroom collectives where mathematics is treated as something worth discussing, taking time over and mathematical ideas as conjectures to be agreed upon. But all of these activities have to be brought to bear on some specific content that we have to plan and carefully select. Variation theory provides a framework for thinking about such content.

What is variation theory?

Variation theory (VT) was developed by Ference Marton and colleagues (Marton, Tsui *et al.* 2004). Marton *et al.* argue that VT is a theory of learning but it is not trying to be an all-encompassing theory. For example, VT makes no claims as to whether or not group work is better than individual work, or whether physical materials are more useful than pictures or images. VT theorists acknowledge that these other features of the learning environment are important (and I deal with the arguments for group work in particular in Chapter 8) but that the aim of VT is to attend to aspects that focus on the specific mathematical content. Thus the drive to develop VT came from the recognition that other theories of learning provide accounts that are independent of the actual content being learned. For instance, advocates of group work as a key component of learning rarely address whether this is equally effective for learning about, say, fractions or measuring angles. Although, as we will see in Chapter 8, while there is evidence for the benefits of group work for particular types of learning (particularly developing understanding) this still does not 'drill down' to the level of particular mathematical topics. As a group of teachers and researchers in Hong Kong engaged in 'learning studies' that draws on VT to look at how diverse classroom communities can learn particular content note:

> Contrary to the belief of some educational theorists, therefore, we believe that one simply cannot develop thinking in isolation from the objects of thought. Learning is always the learning of something, and we cannot talk about learning without paying attention to what is being learnt.
>
> (Lo, Pong *et al.* 2005: 14)

While I find much that resonates in Langer's work on being mindful, it still only provides a broad sense of where we might be heading for in mathematics lessons – it cannot supply specific details for specific topics. VT can fill that gap by drawing our attention to four key features of teaching and learning:

- objects of learning
- critical aspects
- awareness
- discernment and variation.

Objects of learning

VT begins with the acknowledgement of the intentionality of teaching: teaching is always directed toward specific learning ends, or objects. The term 'object' here is not meant to conjure up images of anything physical, but of a desired outcome, much in the sense of subject–object relations in activity theory that I touched on earlier. Despite my claims of the need for teaching to have an element of improvisation, that does not mean that I expect lessons to be lacking in intentions, to be devoid of objects. I do want classes to have learned something by the end of a teaching sequence about symmetry, area, millimeters or whatever. Equally I accept that I cannot completely predict or control the learning outcomes. VT, however, provides a framework for thinking about how to maximize the likelihood of the object of learning being brought into existence.

The object of teaching is not unitary: any teaching activity is always, and inevitably, directed toward at least two objects of learning. There is the specific content of the teaching, the content that is being acted upon such as doubling numbers or plotting graphs, that is, the *direct* object of learning. It is this that learners are usually most focused upon as revealed through their answers to the question 'what did you learn today?' 'How to subtract.' But every teaching activity also encompasses one or more general capabilities that are broader than the specific object of learning, for example, remembering, interpreting, and generalizing. These comprise the *indirect* object of learning (Marton *et al.* ibid.).

There will always be an indirect object of learning to any teaching, even if we have not explicitly planned for this. Since the indirect object is always there, we should pay attention to it – we should be aware, plan and teach for indirect objects. For example, a lesson on multiplying two three-digit numbers together that is based around explicit modeling of the standard algorithm followed by carefully graded practice to ensure 'mastery' of the algorithm has, however implicit or unarticulated, the indirect object of learning committing something to memory and having the resilience and self-discipline to practice this until it is 'second nature'.

Alternatively, a lesson based around long multiplication through modeling calculations as arrays and exploring ways of partitioning these to find solution methods that are suited to the particular numbers in the calculation, could have an indirect object of making calculating a mindful activity.

From the position that learning inevitably goes beyond the mathematics itself, I would go further than Marton and his colleagues and suggest that every teaching activity embodies more than one indirect object of learning, additional objects that are not necessarily mathematical, for example, learning that competition is good, or that some children are naturally 'better' at mathematics than others or that working together can be helpful. As Noddings notes, 'teachers – even when they deny that they do so – transmit something of moral values' (Noddings 2002). Attending primarily to the cognitive in mathematics lessons should not make us blind to the moral values embedded in any lesson. I take up such indirect objects of learning in the next chapter: for the moment I will attend to the specific and general objects of learning mathematics.

Objects of learning are not uniquely specified but, much like the intended, implemented and attained curriculum (see Chapter 3), can be thought of as intended, enacted and lived objects (in the sense of how the individual learner comes to experience the enacted: Marton, Runesson et al. 2004). Although when planning a lesson I may be confident that the objects of learning will be brought into being for the learners, in the actual enactment of the lesson what is attended to may not exactly match my original intentions. Even if the lesson is enacted very much to plan, then the subjective experiences of the learners – the lived object – may result in the outcomes of learning being different from both the intended and the implemented. I recall from early in my teaching planning a history lesson with the specific object of learning about Norman castles and the general object of note taking (although of course I did not use this language to describe my intentions). Everything was enacted much as I planned. We crafted notes about what one might have found in Norman castles, such as 'wooden benches, little other furniture'. Reading the children's essays later I discovered a lived object of learning for most was that the Normans had to put up with sitting on small seats.

Central to examining the links between the intended, enacted and lived objects of learning is the identification of critical aspects.

Critical aspects

Having decided on the intended objects of learning, the critical aspects of these need to be identified. A challenge here is that of 'unpacking' (Ball 1990) the mathematics that we, as adults, have come to accept as unproblematic. For example, adults have no difficulty talking about the fingers (including the thumb) on their hand as five separate fingers or one group of five. For the young learner the shift of unit here from one individual finger to a group of five is far from easy but a critical aspect of being able to count in groups. Without awareness of this critical aspect a child may learn to verbally count in fives but when asked to count a collection of objects may point to them one at a time while counting 'five, ten, fifteen, . . .'. This formation of 'composite units' (Steffe 2002) – five of one or one group of five – can be extended to three levels of units by successive nesting of composite units: for example treating 15 counters organized into three groups of five as a single group of 15 (first level) made up of three units (second level) each of which is made up of five units (third level). Being able to discriminate the different levels of units continues to be a critical aspect beyond simple counting and multiplication: it is a critical aspect for later understanding of fractions. For example, researchers have shown that pupils who can discriminate three-level unit structures develop better understanding of improper fractions (Olive and Steffe 2002).

Consider the following problem adapted from Lamon (2005). 'A bag of sweets contains 20 sweets. That is four fifths of a full bag of sweets. How many sweets in a full bag?' Before reading on try to work out the answer and track the different units you have to deal with.

To arrive at the correct answer of 25 sweets the reasoning goes something along the lines of 'If 20 is four fifths then one fifth must be a quarter of four fifths or one quarter of 20. So one fifth is five and five fifths must be 25.' Look at the different units; one fifth of an unknown unit, one quarter of (the unit) four-fifths, five-fifths as a total unit. It is hardly surprising that many children arrive at 24 as the answer: if 20 are four-fifths then one fifth must be four (you find fifths by dividing by five, $20 \div 5 = 4$).

And that is only one small part of the curriculum. The specialist subject knowledge (Ball and Bass 2003) that teachers need to have to be able to unpack and identify the critical features of the mathematics they teach is far from being fully understood. (Although it is clear that simply having more qualifications in standard mathematics courses does not necessarily equip teachers with this sort of knowledge: Ball and Bass 2000.)

Awareness

Awareness, according to Marton and Booth (1997), has a structure to it. By this they mean that the amount of sensory data that we are subject to cannot all be dealt with at once: some things will be to the foreground of our awareness, others will not. There are some powerful demonstrations of this that you can find on the Internet. I do not want to spoil it for those of you who have not seen any of them, but basically you are asked to attend to something, the result of which is that you become 'blind' to other aspects of what is happening – just search for awareness tests on YouTube. We must try and help learners focus their awareness on critical features. This is done through discernment and variation.

Discernment and variation

Discernment, in VT, is a core process in the emergence of the 'lived' object of learning. According to Bowden and Marton (1998), our lived experience is a result of what we are able to discern, distinguish, and there must be variation in our experiences for this to come about.

> When some aspect of a phenomenon or an event varies while another aspect or other aspects remain invariant, the varying aspect will be discerned. In order for this to happen, variation must be experienced by someone as variation.
>
> (Bowden and Marton 1998: 35)

For example, I have a friend who is a professional musician. Chatting after we have been to concerts together, it is always clear that although we had both been to the same 'enacted' event (sitting in a concert hall with an orchestra playing a symphony), given our different backgrounds and experiences, our 'lived' experiences of the concert are very different. My friend is able to discern things in music, which, although I 'heard' the same thing, I am not able to 'hear'!

Variation is the key to being able to discern. My musician friend can discern things in the music that I am deaf to because of his vastly broader experience of hearing the music, including, in rehearsal, what a poor performance sounds like – an opportunity which radio, concerts and CDs do not provide. The casual listener to music gets little opportunity to experience 'what is not the case'.

> Studies have shown that exposure to variation is critical for the possibility to learn, and that what is learned reflects the pattern of variation that was present in the learning situation.
>
> (Runesson 2005: 72)

How does variation theory help?

Let's look at the example of 'Socks and Sticks' from Chapter 5 through the lens of variation. Typically what gets varied in lessons with simple doubling and halving as the direct object of learning is the numbers in the calculations. This object of learning is likely to be split in two: work on doubling preceding tasks involving halving. These may be presented as simply a page of numerical calculations to work through, or, if put into context, then the range of contexts usually varies along with the numbers. For example, how many gloves in six pairs? How many boots in four pairs? How many socks in five pairs? Variation along these two axes – number and context – is intended to help children 'see through' the contexts to reach a generalized understanding of doubling that is, ultimately, 'context free'. However, all this variation, rather than helping, may result in the lived experience of the learner being different from the intended. A five-year-old may get 'hung up' on what the gloves are made from, whether the boots are wellingtons or fashion, whether the colors of the socks help with sorting them into pairs. No wonder teachers say that contexts only confuse the children and so simply give pages of calculations to work through.

In constructing Socks and Sticks, we kept the variation limited by restricting the number of problems to two, varying the contexts but keeping the two sixes constant, although varying the relationship: doubling in one context and halving 12 in the other. Our intent was that by keeping the numbers invariant, the fact that both situations could be seen as having something to do with 6 + 6 would be brought into the structure of the children's awareness. That they would move from awareness of variation in the contexts – chopsticks and socks – to discerning that there was something common underpinning these. As the discussion about the children's solutions showed, such discernment was not immediate: some children did not see two sixes as a critical feature of each problem, some came to see this as they worked through the problems and a minority were able to immediately discern this. The whole class discussion of the different solutions and the links between these helped some children come to discern this critical feature although I would not go so far as to claim that the lived object of learning was the same for everyone by the end of the lesson.

Constructing examples through variation theory

Working on examples is the bedrock of much mathematics teaching. For many of us that was how we learned mathematics – the practice of doing lots of examples was the main experience of doing mathematics. Some still justify children spending a lot of time working through examples by saying children like it and I can understand why. I loved doing pages of 'sums'. Getting an exercise book of squared paper seemed so grown-up in comparison to the wide-ruled pages of infant school. Setting everything out neatly, one digit to each square, working through and being reasonably confident of getting everything right, then the reward of a full set of red ticks and $^{10}\!\!/\!\!_{10}$ and, joy of joy, a sticky star, made everything in the world seem right and in order. Of course I was one of the lucky ones – I expect my memories and feelings would be very different today if I had struggled to remember the rules, if I'd got pages of crosses and that stomach-churning 'see me' replacing the 'well done'. But I wasn't really engaged in mathematical activity. Pages of sums like this – routinized and easy to do if you have mastered the technique – are closer to knitting than mathematics. I never did manage to master knitting (my stitches always got tighter and tighter) but I still have a great fondness for squared notebooks.

There is, however, still a place for working through examples and this can be of benefit if the children approach them mindfully. Variation theory helps us design examples in ways that maximize the likelihood that they become part of a mindful activity. Consider, for example, these two sets of subtraction calculations that I put together:

Set A	Set B
120 – 90	120 – 90
235 – 180	122 – 92
502 – 367	119 – 89
122 – 92	235 – 180
119 – 89	237 – 182
237 – 182	502 – 367

Set A and Set B both contain the same calculations but in a different order. If you want children to engage with some subtraction calculations, does it make any difference to have these in a particular order? Well, if you want the children only to use one method for subtraction – an algorithmic approach – then it probably doesn't make much difference. Set A provides a collection of practice examples and is typical of what you might find in books of practice examples. But the order of Set B makes it significantly different – the structure of the variation in the calculations as you work through them in order is designed with the expectation of engaging the children in some mindful reasoning. The order of the calculations may prompt the awareness of connections between pairs of calculations and thus reasoning about these. In particular it is designed to try and focus the children's awareness on the mathematical object of 'constant difference': that the difference between a pair of numbers remains constant if the same number is added or subtracted from each number. For example, the difference between 120 and 90 must be the same as the difference between 122 and 92.

A typical way to introduce constant difference would be to state up front that 'today we are learning about constant difference', for the teacher to work through some examples showing why this works and the children then to work through further examples practicing the technique. And therein lies the weakness of this approach. Treating constant difference as a 'technique', a mechanical skill as the OED defines technique. The children's lived object is 'constant difference' as another 'rule' or skill that they have to remember. They are unlikely to engage with it mindfully, and will attend more to the teacher's explanation than to thinking about the mathematics. Thinking about this object of learning through the lens of variation theory provides a way of maximizing engaging mindfully with the big idea that is involved here. A 'mini-lesson' provides the context for this.

Cathy Fosnot has developed a way of whole-class working on examples which seems to me to embody both the principles of variation and mindfulness, in that it requires learners to discern critical features rather than simply treat each calculation afresh (see, for example, Fosnot and Dolk 2001a).

A 'mini-lesson', along the lines of Fosnot's, would be structured around such calculations. The teacher encourages entering the activity mindfully by acting as a vicarious consciousness (Wood, Bruner *et al.* 1976), directing the children to look for and think about possible connections. Let's look at what this might look like in terms of how a teacher could deal with each of the above calculations in turn. The following is a hypothetical example, but it is based on my many experiences of conducting such sessions. The setting would be with the whole class, with around 20 minutes of activity. I am also including some 'asides' about my thinking in the choice of variation. Planning sequences of examples like this is a non-trivial task and the overall shape of the sequence often needs revising in the light of mentally rehearsing how the examples are likely to focus the learners' attention and discernment. The fact that the calculations are presented one at a time allows for the element of improvisation. The teacher can make changes in the enactment of the object of learning in the light of children's responses.

120 – 90   This initial calculation is chosen in the expectation that most children will be able to figure out the answer quite easily. Not a great deal of time would be spent discussing the different methods that they used – agreement is quickly reached that the answer is 30. Note that while any subtraction can be interpreted as taking away or finding the difference, choosing two numbers here that are quite close together I am hoping will nudge the children's attention in the direction of finding the difference. Having asked for answers and agreed on 30 a key teaching move is then to model this subtraction as finding the difference between two points on a number line, as illustrated by Figure 6.1.

Irrespective of how the children actually calculated the answer, awareness is being directed toward the critical feature of difference. (My original choice of example here was 160 – 80 but as I began to work through how this could pan out it became clear that it would be unlikely that children would readily see this as a difference calculation, so I went back and changed the numbers – this mental rehearsal of how each part of lesson relates to what is coming up next is, I think, important.)

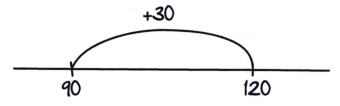

Figure 6.1   120 – 90 as difference

The number line image remains on display as something to refer back to as the calculations unfold. (Japanese classrooms have wall-long whiteboards that are filled over the course of a lesson – the history of the lesson remains on view throughout so that teachers and children can make use of it (Stigler and Hiebert 1999). While virtual flip-charts on interactive whiteboards do allow for 'replay' the child is not in control of this in the way that they can glance back at the record of the lesson.)

122 – 92   I would expect that although having set up the first example as a difference, many children would find the answer to this by taking away 90 from 122 and then taking way the 2 (or taking off the 2 and then the 90). This method could be modeled on the empty number line, but that's not the intention behind this choice of question as next and drawing it could distract the children's awareness away from where I am hoping it is going. Instead I would pose the question 'Why are the answers to these two questions the same? Turn to your neighbor and talk about whether there is a reason for them being the same or if this is just a coincidence.' Their awareness, I hope, is being drawn to the fact that there must be a critical aspect that makes the answers the same (otherwise I would not ask the question!). Back as a collective, we would explore their reasoning; I am expecting that it will emerge that the difference between 122 and 92 must be the same as the difference between 120 and 90 because each number has been increased by the same amount and this moves each of the numbers the same distance along the number line but preserves the difference (Figure 6.2) (hence the reason for modeling the first calculation as difference rather than take-away). Again I would leave this image on the board.

119 – 89   The variation in the example is that each number has been decreased by the same amount, which makes the preservation of the difference not quite so obvious. Some children, however, may already have begun to see what is going on and will quickly know that the answer is still 30. The pedagogical practice of 'thumbs up' rather than 'hands up' is important here. A barrage of hands up in these circumstances sets the wrong tone – the task here is not about speed of getting the answer but about the reasoning through as to why the answer is the same. Holding up a thumb quietly on their laps or tables allows me to see when children are ready without this being distracting to those who are still needing time to figure out the answer. The follow-up conversation here moves more quickly into reasoning through why the same answer has been arrived at again. Again, the image on the empty number line helps make clear what is going on (Figure 6.3)

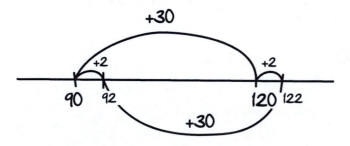

Figure 6.2 122 – 92 as constant difference

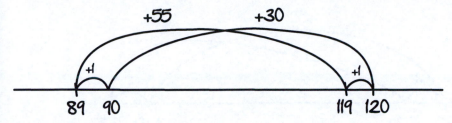

Figure 6.3 119 – 89 as constant difference

235 – 180   The variation here is in the start of a new calculation, with a pair of numbers where the difference between is not quite as easily found as in the first pair. I signal such 'fresh starts' with a change of pen color and a word or two about a new string of calculations, while suggesting to the children that they keep in mind what we have just done. Again I've chosen numbers that are reasonably close together to encourage thinking of the subtraction as finding the difference rather than taking away. After agreeing quite quickly that the answer is 55 it is up there on the empty number line (Figure 6.4).

237 – 182   Rather than asking for the answer to this I would direct the children to think about the first three examples and to look at this example and think about how it is related to 235 – 180. My intent now is to focus their awareness a little more, using the variation in the examples that are still on the board to help. I'd ask them to talk to their neighbor about how they could use the relationship to say quickly what the answer must be and to explain how they know. As before the empty number line provides the support for explaining why the two answers are different (Figure 6.5). By this point in the lesson the language of 'constant difference' can be introduced.

502 – 367   The variation with this final calculation is that the 'anchor' calculation (500 – 365) is not explicitly given. I would be hoping that by now the children are mindful of constant difference and would be aware of seeking out an easier, related, calculation. I encourage the children to write down another calculation that has the same difference. Talking in pairs helps them see that 500 – 365 will have the same difference as 502 – 367. By now some children should be able to come to the front and using the empty number line explain the reason to the rest of the class.

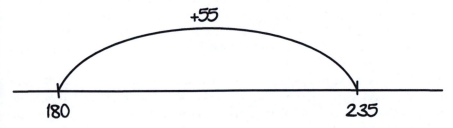

Figure 6.4 235 – 180 as constant difference

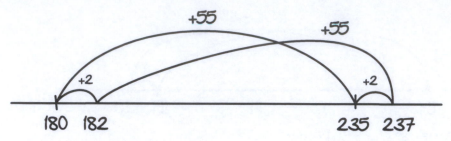

Figure 6.5 237 – 182 as constant difference

There is a key pedagogical decision to make just before this point in the string of calculations based on the teacher's mindfulness of how the children are responding. I have described this here on the assumption that by now the children will be mindful of constant difference on the basis of the examples that we have worked through. But it may be that I was over-optimistic in how quickly they would become aware of this. So at this point in the mini-lesson, the decision may be to put up 500 – 365 rather than go immediately to 502 – 367. The beauty with such 'string' work is that the examples are only going up on the board one at a time. The children don't know what is coming next, so that the shape and direction partly emerge as a result of their responses (I've done lessons where it has taken everyone so long to do 120 – 90 that we have worked on finding differences between multiples of ten instead).

This way of working embodies being 'connectionist' for me – the mathematical ideas that emerge are not totally directed but neither am I expecting the children to 'discover' the idea of constant difference. Building variation into the examples in this way prompts the children to think and reason through what is happening rather than simply try to remember a set routine of how to carry out subtractions. We would be engaging in the activity collectively. Such lessons are neither teacher-centered nor pupil-centered. They are centered around joint mathematical activity.

What is the indirect mathematical object behind introducing constant difference? It is a popularly held view that the reason behind introducing children to a range of calculating strategies is that individual children will have different preferred methods or that one method may make more sense to a child than another. One of my indirect objects is subtly different: it is about choosing the method that is the best for the problem in hand. It isn't really a case of children choosing methods because they find them appealing or the easiest overall to do, but that they are being mindful in selecting the method that is most appropriate for the particular numbers in a particular calculation. Another mini-lesson might start with 120 – 103 and then 120 – 17 to explore when it makes more sense to think of subtraction as 'find the difference' and when it makes more sense to do a 'take-away'.

But there is another indirect object to such calculations and that is to engage children in mindful mathematical activity. Lessons like this are not just about being able to calculate correct answers. They are about inducting children into mathematics as a meaningful, collective, endeavor.

Variation and looking for patterns

I hope that the above account shows that discerning connections and patterns is not simply a case of trying out lots of different examples until some underlying repetition becomes clear. Pattern finding is an activity that involves looking at the variation between items, adjacent pairs in particular, and trying to discern a connection that has some underlying structure.

All too often we focus on the number patterns and assume that that is sufficient. For example, think about the pattern of the multiples of five. Children quickly learn that numbers ending in zero or five are multiples of five, but are less often invited to think through and be mindful of why this may be so. Directing awareness here is not that difficult: ten is a multiple of five, so any multiple of ten is also going to be a multiple of five, hence all numbers ending in zero are multiples of five. Numbers ending in five are five more than a multiple of ten, so these must also be a multiple of five. Why bother going to these lengths? Well, this reasoning extends to other multiples. Numbers ending in even digits, two, four, six, or eight, are multiples of two because, beyond ten, we can think of them as multiples of ten plus a multiple of two. For example $176 = 170 + 6$. Since ten is a multiple of two, all multiples of ten are multiples of two, add a multiple of two to a multiple of ten and the result will be a multiple of two.

Later on children may encounter the 'rule' that, for three-digit and larger numbers, if the last two digits are a multiple of four, then the whole number is a multiple of four. Why? By the same logic, we are partitioning the number into a multiple of 100 and a multiple of four, for example, $1456 = 1400 + 56$, since any multiple of 100 is a multiple of four, both are multiples of four and so must be the sum. You might like to think about how this extends to becoming mindful of how to check if a number is a multiple of eight.

I used the word 'rule' above but we want children to be aware that in mathematics 'rules' are not arbitrary, in the way that they can be in everyday life. For example, we have the rules of the road: stop at red lights; drive on the right and so forth. But some countries drive on the left and we could all have traffic lights where you had to stop on blue. Nothing essentially requires cars to be on the right, or to stop on red (other than the chaos that would follow if the rules were not obeyed). Mathematical 'rules' – multiples of five end in five or zero – are not arbitrary or rooted in convention but based in mathematical structure.

Mindless pattern spotting

Pattern spotting without being mindful of the underlying structure that is giving rise to the pattern can lead the learner astray. Here is a classic example:

Draw a circle and mark one dot on the circumference. With only one dot on the circumference there is one region within the circle. Adding a second dot and joining the two dots results in two regions within the circle.

What happens to the number of regions as the number of dots increases? Positioning the dots so that the maximum number of regions is created results in the following pattern:

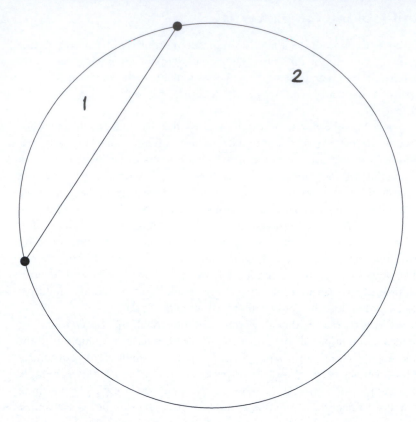

Figure 6.6 Two dots, two regions

Dots	Regions
1	1
2	2
3	4
4	8
5	16

Figure 6.7 shows the diagram for five dots and the resulting 16 regions. Note that the dots are not equally spaced around the circumference of the circle: if they were there is a possibility that three lines will all cross at the same point and so fewer than 16 regions would be created. We want the maximum number of regions.

Before reading on, what is your prediction for the maximum number of regions for six dots? If you have paper and pencil to hand you might like to check your prediction by quickly sketching a circle, mark in the dots irregularly around the circumference and join them all up.

Did you predict 32 regions? Did you manage to draw the circle and regions and create the 32? It's hard to do this and when I present this problem in workshops teachers will often spend quite a bit of time adjusting the diagram to get the 32 regions and many convince themselves that they have found them all.

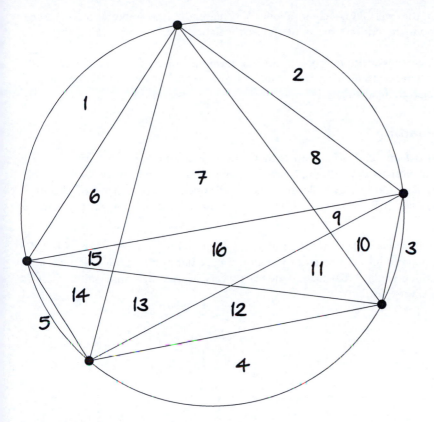

Figure 6.7 Five dots, sixteen regions

In fact, although it looks like the underlying pattern is doubling, it isn't. For six dots the maximum number of regions is 31 not 32. No matter where you position the dots around the circumference, only 31 regions are ever possible. So powerful is the impression from the table that the pattern must be doubling that I've had people argue that I'm wrong and they have found 32 regions. Very close inspection reveals this not to be the case, but shaking off that initial pattern is difficult.

The numbers in the table only reflect the underlying structure of what is emerging – they do not determine it. Yet often pattern spotting is left at the level of drawing conclusions from tables like this – the next stage of establishing what is going on that results in these figures is not addressed. (Incidentally the underlying structure in the joining the dots investigation is subtle and beyond the scope here.)

Summary

Variation theory provides a structure for thinking through how to plan lessons that maximize the chance that the children's lived object of mathematical learning is close to the teacher's intended object. By helping teachers think through the links between the intended, enacted and lived objects of learning, it can help us try to align these without assuming that this will always come about. VT highlights the importance of teacher knowledge about the critical aspects of the mathematics and how unpacking this is far from trivial.

VT also draws our attention to the indirect learning objects, with regard to mathematical competencies. In the next two chapters I turn to look at indirect learning objects that are less directly mathematical.

Further reading

Young Mathematicians at Work materials by Cathy Fosnot and colleagues. This is a rich vein of mathematical activity. Although not developed through the lens of VT the books and resources that Cathy and colleagues have developed embody many of the ideas discussed here. Search Fosnot on the USA Heinemann website to track all the materials down.

For Each and Everyone edited by Lo Mun Ling, Pong Wing Yan and Pakey Chik Pui Man. This book goes into the detail of variation theory but also looks at the application of this in 'learning studies' that take particular objects of learning and examine these in classrooms of diverse learners.

Chapter 7

Transforming the learner

What creates natural laughter? The unexpected, the spontaneous, giving without thought of return, falling down and getting up, being playful, being silly – these things can bring joy. Create a space where there are no wrong answers. Hang out there.

(Madson 2005)

It's not often that I do demonstration lessons, as I feel it's important to know the children you're working with and the sort of classroom culture that they are used to working within. The established culture may not be conducive to the way I want to work with the children and my expectations for how they could work together. Working cooperatively is a skill that needs to be honed over time and if children's mathematical experiences have been largely based around working individually, then my lessons are less likely to be models of the sort of practice I aspire to, more likely to be disasters and reinforce views of 'see, I always knew these kids can't work together'.

However, on one occasion, I owed a friend a favor and agreed to conduct a lesson with a group of ten-year-old children who had come together from several different schools. There were about 30 children in all, three or four from each school. We started off playing some counting games in a circle and then I assigned the children to random groups of four or five. That was probably my big mistake. I had hoped that the children would quickly bond in their new groups and work effectively together. However, it was not to be. I set up the problem for them to work on – it doesn't matter what it was – and encouraged the children to work in pairs or trios on coming up with a solution. I provided only one piece of paper and one pencil between twos and threes in order, I hoped, to further encourage collaboration.

As the children began on the activity, I worked my way slowly round the groups taking note of what they were doing, encouraging them and giving assistance where needed. Eventually I came to the table where there were five children: three boys and two girls. A boy and a girl were sitting together and two boys and the other girl were on the opposite side of the table. The boy–girl pair had positioned themselves so that the boy had the paper in front of him while the girl was facing away from him. In the trio, the two boys had sat themselves in such a way that the girl could not see the paper at all that they were working on. I, a bit grumpily, said, 'Come on folks, I asked you to work together.' One of the boys from the trio responded, 'I don't need to work with anyone.' Even more irked, I retorted, 'I don't care what you think you need I want you to work together.' As you might expect, this had rather the opposite effect to the one that I intended.

What was particularly galling, and the main contribution to my grumpiness, was that sitting at the same table as these children was a head teacher who had watched this behavior unfold and, it seemed given his lack of intervention, thought that it was all quite acceptable. Talking later to the colleague who had set the session up, she suggested that such a reaction was not untypical of schools in that area.

This example epitomizes what my colleague, Jeremy Hodgen, describes as the creeping culture of 'maths at any price'. It seems that with the relentless focus on test results and, in England, whether or not end of primary schooling targets are being met, means that other aspects of the curriculum, particularly the social and emotional, might be side-lined within mathematics lessons. In this chapter I look at the arguments that challenge this view.

Beyond the mathematics

The primary aim of every teacher must be to promote the growth of students as competent, caring, loving and lovable people. Teachers with this aim will work flexibly in teaching mathematics – inspiring those who care about mathematics for itself to inquire ever more deeply, helping those who care instrumentally about mathematics to prepare for the line of work they desire, and supporting as best they can those students who wish they never had to encounter mathematics. To have uniformly high expectations for all students in mathematics is morally wrong and pedagogically disastrous. It is part of a sloganized attempt to make our schools look democratic and egalitarian, when in fact they are systems continually struggling for tighter control.

(Noddings 2005: 154)

Noddings throws down quite a challenge. Amid reports that lack of mathematical qualifications are correlated with poor employment opportunities there are some who would say that not having high expectations for everyone would be a dereliction of a teacher's moral duty. For example, a major study (Brynner and Parsons 1997) drew this conclusion on data from the National Child Development Study (NCDS), a large-scale longitudinal study of a sample of UK citizens born in a single week in 1958. These people have been followed through to adult life and at age 37, a 10 percent sample of the original cohort (1,714 people) were interviewed and tested on literacy and numeracy skills. While 70 percent of this sample was deemed competent in both literacy and numeracy, the evidence revealed that those people with poor numeracy skills had left school early, often without qualifications, and had more difficulty getting and maintaining full-time employment and those who were in employment were generally in poorly paid, low-grade jobs with limited prospects.

Women in particular, with low levels of numeracy, were more likely to be excluded from jobs that they saw as desirable. The reason for this, the researchers argue, is that the sorts of employment that young women want to go into require increasingly sophisticated numeracy skills: given the changes in the technology since 1997, this situation can only have got more extreme. While mathematics may be disappearing from our day-to-day lives on the high street, workplaces increasingly require numerate staff.

We need to be cautious in conflating correlation with causality here: low levels of numeracy may be correlated with poor job prospects, but raising levels of numeracy may not guarantee access to jobs: mathematics is typically a 'gate-keeper' qualification for entry into some positions. Increase the number of people with the qualification and the 'bar' may simply be raised. Nevertheless, the evidence is that jobs increasingly demand numeracy skills and lack of these is likely to be a barrier to such employment.

So there is a moral tension here: preparing the learner for their future career prospects as well as developing qualities of being caring and loving. It is tempting to 'bracket off' the latter on the argument that mathematical understanding has to take priority in the mathematics lessons and the 'touchy-feely' stuff can be done at other times. I do not find this argument tenable. First, because such bracketing off is impossible – children are going to be learning about themselves and others in mathematics lessons whether we intend them to or not. Second, because the research shows that attending to relationships in mathematics lessons actually helps to raise standards, not to lower them (Boaler 1999).

Noddings's main argument is directed at secondary schools, so it may be that it does not apply to primary. I find it helpful to think about having high expectations at primary school as 'leveling the playing field'. A main aim of Japanese primary mathematics is based on the recognition that inequality of attainment in the primary years may be more a result of children's different experiences than their 'innate' mathematical ability. Thus the emphasis is on bringing all pupils up to a level of competency, rather than take the spread of attainment as a necessary given and an indication that some children are already mathematically 'less able' (National Institute on Student Achievement 1998). While the cost of this may be a slight diminution of the standards of the higher attaining pupils at the end of primary school, this seems worth paying for everyone entering secondary school to be at the same starting gate. And a further gain is the higher average attainment of all primary school pupils. Once in secondary school the 'gifted and talented' have the opportunity to 'inquire ever more deeply' as Noddings puts it. As Susan Hart points out, the issue is not one of whether or not some children are more 'able' than others but the impact of acting as though that is the case (Hart 1998).

Note that Noddings is not talking about mathematical ability but learners' relationship to the subject. It is important therefore that primary mathematics provides children with as much of a taste of genuine mathematical activity as it can so that they can know whether or not they have an appetite for it. Kath Cross reports David Wheeler as once saying:

> I don't expect, and I don't want, all children to find mathematics an engrossing study, or one that they want to devote themselves to either in school or in their lives. Only a few will find mathematics seductive enough to sustain a long-term engagement. But I would hope that all children could experience at a few moments in their careers . . . the power and excitement of mathematics . . . so that at the end of their formal education they at least know what it is like and whether it is an activity that has a place in their future.
>
> (Cross 2004)

In the previous chapters I have set out some of the ways that I think primary mathematics can be taught that could maximize children getting a sense of the power of mathematics:

by thinking about learning as a complex activity rather than a series of actions; by encouraging children to develop a mindful attitude to mathematics; by using variation theory to plan for awareness. In this chapter I explore Noddings's point, which I firmly agree with, that mathematics education can help pupils learn about themselves and their relationships. In other words I am turning attention to the interpretation of 'transforming mathematics education' as the power of mathematics education to transform the learner, and not just in terms of coming to know some mathematics.

Learning that is transformational in the sense that I examine here is risky. But by providing mathematical challenges that encourage children to take risks and a trusting classroom community that provides support for that risk, then I suggest that mathematics education can do much more to promote 'healthy' learners than it currently does.

Learning as a transformative experience

Learning to ride a bicycle is a transformative experience for children who are lucky enough to have the opportunity. The move from a tricycle to a two-wheeler with 'stabilizers' is an important transition, bringing the ownership of a 'real' bike into sight. I still remember my first grown-up bike: a red 'chopper' that was state of the art for the 1960s. Being given this bike was significant in many ways. I didn't simply become 'Mike-with-a-bike': I joined a community of bike-riders and became friends with 'the gang'. With that came both opportunities and challenges. Opportunities to be more independent, to travel further, to have adventures. Such opportunities were not unproblematic and, in particular, they presented challenges to my relationship with my parents. While I was excited at the new-found freedoms my bike brought me, they were concerned about safety. I enjoyed going off with the gang, they worried about not knowing where I was. Becoming a bike-rider was a transformative experience, for the whole family.

We do not often think and talk about learning mathematics in this transformative sense. Instead we tend to talk about learning maths in ways that suggest it is simply an additive process: the Mary who learns long multiplication is essentially the same Mary that she was before except now she 'has' long multiplication. She has 'added' some maths to her repertoire of skills and knowledge, but Mary, in essence, is untouched, has not been fundamentally transformed.

Resistance to mathematics

Part of this keeping separate the 'essence' of the learner from the 'knowledge' of mathematics arises from the language of 'delivering' content that I talked about in Chapter 3. I also think that most people have a poor and limiting image of what it means to become mathematically successful. The everyday language that we use is not exactly flattering to mathematicians. Being 'calculating' or being 'rational' are hardly used as compliments. Indeed there is a body of research that considers mathematics education to be a major contributor to the maintenance of a male-dominated patriarchal society that requires suppression of emotion and of concerns with the world of relationships (see the work of Valerie Walkerdine in particular here (1988)).

A root difficulty here is the idea that mathematics education need only, and is only, concerned with the production of a disinterested rational understanding of the discipline – that learning mathematics is separated and insulated from learning anything else and particularly from learning about yourself (or others). As the 'standards and back-to-basics' debates reveal, many buy into the 'additive' model of learning maths. How you teach it doesn't really matter, it just needs to be learnt. Even many attempts to make maths 'fun' still only really attend to 'getting the maths across' rather than addressing what the learner is becoming in this process.

From the young learners' perspective, however, the overarching focus of school life is largely about learning about yourself. Am I popular? Am I smart? Can I do maths? Do I want to do maths? One unintended consequence of this mismatch between the seemingly single goal of teaching – just to learn some maths – and the goal of learning – finding out about me – is that learners think that they are learning about themselves when in fact they are learning about the shortcomings and limitations of the way that mathematics is taught. Look at the number of times that people, teachers included, say 'oh I was never any good at maths'. People never say 'oh I was never any good at walking' because it is accepted that, physical handicaps aside, everyone can and will learn to walk. It is less of a given that everyone can learn mathematics.

Learning about oneself

It is not fashionable these days to talk about learning as building character. We prefer the language of 'independent learners' or 'engaged citizens' but the construct of character is still present in this rhetoric in the sense of 'the collective qualities or characteristics, esp. mental and moral, that distinguish a person' (OED). Mental and moral. Allowing boys in a group to subjugate girls is a dereliction of our moral duty as teachers. Pursuit of the mental must not drive out the moral.

I do not want talk of character to be confused with the sense of developing 'strength of character' through the application of will and grit. The old 'if it was good enough for me lad, then it's good enough for you' argument. There always seems to be the hint of this behind calls for a return to 'basics' – that 'applying yourself' to learning long division builds 'moral fiber'. Not only is there no reason to suppose that learning through drill and practice actually does produce generalizable, transferable 'grit', there is ample evidence that it turns people away from mathematics (Boaler 1997).

Neither am I suggesting that learning maths must always be made easy or that it does not occasionally need the application of a bit of grit. It is that such grit needs to be applied mindfully and directed at something meaningful rather than pages of exercises. Children of all ages can demonstrate remarkable powers of concentration when the task in hand has captured their interest. They don't have to draw on 'will power' to play for an hour on the Wii or to work on mimicking their favorite pop-star's dance routine: the pleasure in the activity itself provides the motivation. Pleasure can be found in mathematical activity. It is pleasure in the form of 'flow' as the psychologist Mihaly Csikszentmihalyi puts it (1990). People reporting themselves as in a state of 'flow' – being fully absorbed in their present activity – do not necessarily report themselves as having fun or that the activity is easy. In fact the sense of pleasure may be experienced after the activity is finished, in looking back over it at the time.

Getting into 'flow' is a balance of challenge with one's sense of current levels of competence. Activities that are easy and well within our competence do not engage us too much, while a level of challenge that seems beyond one's current capability is disabling. You find yourself in the flow with an optimum level of challenge that stretches your capabilities. For me, such states are best engendered in mathematics classrooms through paired work. A pair of children can be given a challenge that is more difficult than either can do on their own and, in a supportive environment, both 'rise' to the level of the challenge. This means that we have to plan challenges that are at a higher level of difficulty than we would present to a child on their own. Simply pitching the work at the same level of difficulty that you would give to the individual child is less likely to engage the pair of children in 'flow'. In those circumstances, paired work then only serves the purpose of making the activity more pleasant to engage in; it is less likely to develop both children's thinking. 'Jellybeans' (see Chapter 2) is typical of what can emerge when the level of challenge for pairs is beyond what the children could have done individually. We were at the point of working with that class where we could challenge them with something like this and they would go 'hey, that's hard' and we could say, 'Yes, but have a go.' The payoff here is more than just higher standards. These children came to view themselves as mathematicians: maths was a subject that they could not only do but wanted to do. They came to care for and care about mathematics.

In professional development sessions I often show teachers the Jellybeans example and while they are impressed, many will say 'My kids could not do that'. They are probably right. The children who did do it probably would not have been able to if 'Jellybeans' had simply been a 'one-off' activity, if we had not been working with them for some time. That is why mathematical activity has to be looked at historically (in the small-scale sense of the history of this class) as well as culturally and socially. These were not particularly gifted children from privileged backgrounds. The equivalent class in the school the year before most certainly could not have solved such problems. But we had worked with these children for 18 months, we had built up a classroom culture that emphasized listening to each other, working together and trying things out rather than waiting for the teacher to provide help. And, most importantly, the children trusted us and their peers that in sharing their attempts at solutions to difficult problems they would be treated respectfully. Sharing solutions was used to help everyone better understand the mathematics rather than simply being judged on being right or wrong and in doing so created a trusting community.

This took time. An incident early on in our work in the school illustrates the history of building these ways of working. With a class of eight-year-olds we had put a calculation on the board and asked them to figure out the answer and share it with their neighbor. Figuring it out was OK, but the sharing was a nightmare. The children were hugely resistant to sharing with each other. It seemed the children would much rather poke each other with pencils than listen to each other. In the circumstances it would have been easy to fall into 'if only . . .' thinking: 'it's these children. If only they behaved better then we could get them sharing.'

What we actually did was look at what we could do differently, while still keeping in mind the ultimate indirect object of children being able to work effectively in pairs. We began by asking ourselves why there was such a gap between the children's lived object of the lesson and our intended object. While we believed that working cooperatively would benefit the pairs of children, their lived experience of this was that there was nothing to be gained from listening to a partner's explanation – 'what is the point of listening to you, I've got the answer' and much to be lost from explaining – 'why should I "give away" my solution?' Looked at from their perspective we could ask ourselves how to change this lived experience from this lose-lose one to win-win. We developed a sequence of paired activities that, from the children's perspective, made more human sense. For example, a simple initial change we made was to put up two calculations and each child in the pair to answer one or the other. Now when sharing solutions they weren't 'giving anything away' to their partner and in listening they were hearing something that was new. (There are more details about this in Chapter 10.) The class did come to be able to work effectively in pairs but it took several months to get there. This is another reason why we need to set our indirect objects beyond the lesson or week. Building classroom community is an ongoing project, as I discuss in the next chapter.

The time spent on the ways of working collectively in order to raise the level of challenge did pay off. When the children in the 'Jellybeans' class came to do their end of year National Tests they reported finding them easy and the high results confirmed this: when they had to work individually the level of challenge was lower than they had been used to and they did well.

A review of research by Peter Kutnick and colleagues confirms the power of paired work (2005). Their findings show that working in pairs is most effective for helping children develop understanding. Interestingly his research also shows that paired work is not necessarily always the best arrangement. When it comes to practice activities – fluency – they argue that working individually is most effective. Paired work can actually get in the way of getting on with practicing. If practice directed at fluency (that is, children are practicing what they already can do in order to keep skills sharp, much as musicians practice scales), then perhaps that's best set for homework rather than precious classroom time being given over to it. Small-group work (four to six pupils) seems best suited to extension practices. The different suitabilities of different groupings to different learning objects indicates that we need to develop a 'social pedagogy' (Kutnick, Blatchford *et al.* 2002) that matches grouping to teaching objects.

Dealing with emotions

Noddings (2002) warns against favoring detached, rational thinking over emotion and inspiration. Drawing on the work of C. S. Lewis she argues that setting aside the emotional in education means a lack of satisfaction of 'the innate longing that most students have for matters that seize the heart' (p. 70). Can mathematics 'seize the heart'? Gauss reported being 'seized' by mathematics and as Bertrand Russell said:

> At the age of eleven, I began Euclid, with my brother as my tutor. This was one of the great events of my life, as dazzling as first love. I had not imagined there was anything so delicious in the world. From that moment until I was thirty-eight, mathematics was my chief interest and my chief source of happiness.
>
> (Russell 2000)

These responses from Gauss and Russell seem to link to what might be described as 'psychic rewards' of engagement with mathematics. Writing several years ago, Lortie talked of the psychic rewards of teaching; the joys and satisfactions arising from caring for and working with others. This was certainly one of the things that attracted me to teaching. Now, some 30 years later, I still think it is important to bring some element of uncertainty to mathematics lessons, to tap into young learners' delight in rising to a challenge. As Fullan and Hargreaves put it: 'These psychic rewards of teaching are important. They are central to sustaining teachers' sense of value and worth in their work' (1996).

Equally important as the psychic rewards of teaching are the psychic rewards of learning. In a culture of learning mathematics being broken down into lesson-sized learning objectives, pre-determined and pre-digested, when do learners get a chance to experience:

- the delight of making a connection
- the pleasure of tussling with a problem
- the fascination of finding short cuts
- the joy of an elegant solution?

Psychic rewards do not come about without effort, they are not 'fluffy' experiences. They come about through engagement with the mathematics. And engagement may be effortful and mindful.

When the emotional aspects of learning mathematics are discussed they tend to be in terms of making the maths 'fun'. If by 'fun' we mean playful, then yes, 'the play's the thing'.

What makes things playful? A common property of what we describe as 'play' – games in particular – is an unknown outcome. The fun from watching sport being played is the degree of unpredictability: look at the lengths that some people go to not to learn the outcome of a match if they have to watch a re-run. Popular TV from reality shows to murder mysteries ('plays') holds your attention partly through the unpredictability of the outcomes. Even young children, playing at mummies or daddies or 'school', have an unpredictableness to the 'scripts' they are playing out. Part of fun, enjoyment, is not knowing what comes next. So where is the fun in being told what you are going to learn in a lesson? Where is the fun and pleasure in a lesson that is so tightly scripted that you know exactly what is coming next? Playing safe does not lead to fun.

Anyone who has ever seen me teach will know my 'style' is quite informal and marked by a lot of laughter – I think we do have fun, but it's more about the relationships we are establishing, relationships that allow us safely to admit when we are lost, that allow us to get it wrong and be laughed with rather than at and a tone of 'let's muddle through all this together'.

Difficult emotions

While positive emotions are generally regarded as a good thing in mathematics classrooms, negative emotions are more often treated as a problem to be 'managed'. I think there is a dark side to the desire to make maths fun, and that is the hope that by making maths fun any uncomfortable aspects will be eliminated. We have a problem in the way that we separate the emotional from the cognitive: we separate out 'managing behavior' from managing the mathematics. I've been in many classrooms that try to operate some sort of behaviorist management of children's acceptable actions, for example, a poster of a ladder that children's names are placed on and moved up or down according to whether or not actions are acceptable, or a traffic light system along the lines that are similar to yellow or red cards in football matches. Children go 'off task' and suddenly it's their fault – they move from green to amber on the traffic lights of behavior. Or get a yellow card, or lose a house point or whatever. But most of the time such 'off-task' behavior is not simply the 'property' of the child. Even when a class is having 'fun' how often we tell them to 'settle down' and get on with the maths. We cannot treat emotions as though they are somehow separate from the maths or getting in the way of it. Cognition and affect are dialectically linked. Children's emotional responses may be distinguishable from their cognitive but they are not separate.

While not denying that some children may have emotional issues that make it difficult for them to fit into classrooms and that some such techniques may be needed to maintain order in a room of 30, we need to be careful not to confuse difficulty with emotions generally with the difficult emotions that can arise in the course of mathematical activity. Learning maths is sometimes difficult and challenging, sometimes a bit of gritting of teeth is needed, and sometimes there is dull practice to do. Children will react to these experiences, but do not have the self-awareness to say 'Excuse me miss, I'm feeling uncomfortable because I'm finding this difficult or I don't understand.' They will deal with their uncomfortable feelings in ways that may diminish the feeling for the individual but are seen as disruptive to others.

Engaging with mathematics is not always a pleasant affair. Any worthwhile mathematical experience is going to lead at times to some difficult emotions surfacing: frustration, confusion and irritation. I've lost track of the number of times that teachers have asked me how maths can be taught so that children don't get confused. They generally aren't too happy with my response that confusion is a necessary part of learning mathematics and can never be removed from the process.

James Nottingham talks about the 'pit of confusion' that children need to enter into when learning (2010). Rather than trying to manage the difficult emotions that arise when in this 'pit', better to share with children that this is a normal and expected part of learning the mathematics. Better to stop the class and talk about the tensions in the air, to reassure them that these are normal and acceptable feelings and that together they can be worked through. Mathematics education can have a transformative effect in helping young learners accept that difficult and uncomfortable feelings are not 'bad' and have to be 'removed' or 'controlled' but that they have to be lived with and worked through and that this is a normal part of learning that everyone goes through. But that can only come about within a supportive and trusting community.

I want to point to the difference between an 'ethic of care', as Noddings would put it, and 'taking care of'. There is a lot of 'taking care of' in teaching, particularly in terms of taking care not to expose children to mathematics that might prove difficult or challenging. A caring relationship is not the same as a cosseting relationship. Like anything worth learning, maths requires effort and we are doing children a disservice if we don't help them appreciate this. Effort has some unwarranted bad connotations and attempts to avoid it – breaking maths down into bite-sized chunks, trying to make it mindless fun – are not helpful. Maths is not bitter medicine that needs to be sugared.

Summary

My particular philosophy of education is important to me, and I am committed to it for my own practice. *But the living other is more important than any theory*, and my theory must be subordinate to the caring relationship.

(Noddings 2005: xviii, original emphasis)

I would add that, in addition to taking priority over any theory, the living other must be more important than any set of government-imposed targets. I've sat in on 'booster' lessons where the children look like rabbits in headlights, clearly terrified of the mathematics and panic stricken.

I want to caution against equating attending to the 'living other' as education about being focused on the individual. The living society is also more important than any theory. It's not just the individual child that we need to care for, but also the society that education is helping to shape.

Although one cannot really be 'intimate' with mathematics as the object of the relation is not another person, mathematics, strictly speaking, has no affect toward us; it cannot reciprocate by caring back. But people do talk as though such a thing were possible. We might not be able to have all children fall in love with mathematics, but we might convince them that it is worth caring about.

Further reading

The Challenge to Care in Schools by Nel Noddings. You may have gathered that I am a big fan of Noddings's work. That may be because before turning to writing about educational philosophy more generally her work was within mathematics education.

Experiencing School Mathematics by Jo Boaler. Although most of Boaler's research is in secondary schools, her findings and messages are equally applicable to primary mathematics. Anyone particularly interested in why girls get turned off maths will find her work particularly helpful.

Chapter 8

Building mathematical community

A sense of belonging, of continuity, of being connected to others and to ideas and values that make our lives meaningful and significant – these needs are shared by all of us.

(Thomas J. Sergiovanni 1999)

We tend to value personal virtues and qualities in discussing what contributes to learning mathematics, for example resilience, perseverance and curiosity. While not denying the importance of these, we also need to acknowledge the importance of relational qualities such as trust, friendliness, inclusion and acceptance of diversity. Some theorists go so far as to argue that relationships and relational values are more important than individual attributes. That we are who we are through our relationships. Kenneth Gergen is a theorist who argues that the particular 'psychology' that we have (that is the discipline of psychology – the science of who we are as individuals) only has the emphasis on the individual as a result of the history of the discipline and that a psychology that was based on relationships could have been the one that grew up and would have been perhaps a more powerful one in helping us understand ourselves (a good starting point for exploring this is Gergen 2009).

Previously I suggested that part of the attraction of learning to ride a bike is the desire to become part of the community of bike-riders. Do current classroom practices establish mathematical classroom communities that are inviting and make children want to join them? As I also pointed out, popular talk about being mathematical is not enticing and the media do not present communities of mathematicians as being particularly inviting. For example, the popular film *Good Will Hunting* presented a hero who could not be a serious mathematician and get the girl. It is important that classroom communities are established in ways that counteract such images and make mathematics inviting, engaging, welcoming and inclusive. Many current practices are not inclusive – you are either good at maths or not – and many children come to regard mathematics as a community that excludes them.

Another reason for paying more attention to community is to balance the focus on the individual that I discussed in Chapter 2. The dominant emphasis in much of the current discourse on mathematics education (particularly, but not exclusively, in England) is predicated on 'fixing' individual pupils. Are individuals making adequate progress, and if not, what provision is being made for them? Any community that emerges out of this seems to be assumed to take form 'naturally'. It's a bit like assuming that if you can make bricks then you can build a cathedral. In this chapter I argue that there is a dialectical relationship between individuals and community. Community is more than the sum of the individuals making it up. By attending to the vision of what we want our mathematical classroom communities to look like, and by making these inviting to individuals, then not only can mathematical learning be improved but also the social world of the child.

Community or organization?

Children in school are organized into classes, but are these classes always communities? Communities are built upon a sense of belonging and this needs to be continuously built. Community is not simply the result of putting a group of people into the same room. There is a tendency to separate off community building and strengthening activities from the mathematics curriculum – learning maths has to be the priority of lessons. I am arguing that attending to community building within lessons can 'kill two birds': improve the mathematics learning and build classroom community.

Some myths about community

Community building depends on conformity

One reason why we don't pay more attention to building community in mathematics classes is because of some myths around the idea. These include thinking that community building relies on individual conformity. Attending to community is not about promoting conformity; it is not about making everyone the same. Successful communities thrive on diversity. They also draw on people's strengths. Building a successful community means recognizing and using the mathematical strengths learners bring to the classroom, not looking at what they cannot do and trying to fill gaps. Looking at classrooms through the lens of complexity theory indicates that diversity is actually a key catalyst in the emergence of ideas (Davis and Sumara 2006).

Community building is done at times other than within mathematics lessons

This is based on a perspective of community as container. That there is this 'thing' the 'classroom community' that 'holds' the mathematics lesson. If these – community and content of lessons – are separate then they can be 'fashioned' separately, just as a potter can make a bowl independently of making some soup that might go in the bowl. In that sense, making the bowl and cooking the soup are both technical problems that can be attended to separately.

Community building, however, is not a technical problem but an adaptive one (Heifetz, Linsky *et al.* 2009). Building community is only solved through the building of it. Community cannot be 'managed' into being, it has to emerge. And this has to be a continuous process. This is important in the building of mathematical classroom communities as generating and sharing ideas involves risk taking and this in turn requires a supportive community, a theme that I return to when discussing talk in Chapter 11.

The writer Thomas Sergiovanni distinguishes between two different types of community. Drawing on German concepts he makes the distinction between community values and contractual values. Community values embody commitment to the community, obligations and duties that arise toward each other by a shift from 'I' to 'we' and bonding through common goals and shared values (Sergiovanni 1999: 6). In German such communities are referred to as gemeinschaft.

In contrast there are groups where shared goals and values are replaced by contractual requirements – gesellschaft. Such groups are marked by politeness rather than actual concern for others. In exploring the differences between gemeinschaft and gesellschaft, Sergiovanni draws on the work of Tönnies who in turn distinguishes between natural will and rational will (ibid. p. 9). Natural will is the motivation for creating community where relationships within the community exist simply because people want to relate to each other, there is no goal or ulterior motive behind coming together. Rational will on the other hand is when people relate to each other in order to gain mutual benefit or achieve some goal.

Classrooms do not allow children to decide whether or not they come together as a community through natural will: as a child you have no choice over your classmates. So there is always going to be a degree of rational will operating in lessons. But we can nevertheless work toward building and creating shared goals and values in the mathematics classroom – gemeinschaft – rather than imposing rules and regulations that create an orderly class but not a community – gesellschaft. In doing so children can learn about how and why they might want to live with others. The moral and the mathematics come together.

Community of memory

Bellah and colleagues (1985), in discussion of what makes for a community, emphasize the history of the community and the 'community of memory' (p. 323) that this engenders. We have to ask ourselves what sort of 'community of memory' is being created through our current practices in teaching mathematics. The dominant 'unit' of mathematics activity is the lesson – learning is seen to be bounded by a unit of time of around an hour. First of all we know that learning needs periods of incubation – over more time – but such short units of activity and engagement do not make for a strong community of memory. There may be the collective memory that lessons involved writing down the learning objective for the day, teacher explaining what to do and then working on tasks, but ask children to recall what stands out for them in terms of memories about the mathematics itself and very little is forthcoming. In fact some popular practices may unintentionally militate against building collective memory. For example, using individual whiteboards may encourage children to try out things. However, if we accept that building memory is not simply an individual internal cognitive act but relies upon shared artifacts then the lack of permanent records of mathematical activity reduces the resources available for building collective memory.

Effects of classroom grouping practices

Styles of working

If we are to attend to developing community within the course of mathematics teaching then we need to think about the impact of practices within the mathematics lessons that go beyond the learning of mathematics. For example, most of the research into collaborative group work in mathematics focuses on the advantages (or not) of this way of working on mathematical learning outcomes. Research outside mathematics education helps us to also consider the impact of grouping practices on the formation of the classroom community and the impact this may have on learners' subsequent activity.

The researchers Keenan and Carnevale (1989) have examined the impacts of cooperative versus competitive group work from the perspective of the sorts of relationships created through these ways of working, not just the learning outcomes. Although their research is with older students I can see no reason to think that primary pupils would respond any differently. In one of their studies, groups were assigned tasks that were set up to encourage the group either to work cooperatively or to work competitively. The researchers were interested in the effect that these different ways of working – the 'in-group style' as they dubbed it – would have on subsequent interactions with other groups – the 'out-group' interactions. In particular they were interested in whether the in-group style would be replicated when groups subsequently had to work with other groups, or whether a different style of working would emerge. They posited two different possible hypothetical outcomes related to each style of in-group working. With regard to the groups that initially worked cooperatively, the researchers hypothesized that when these groups worked with another group they might relate to the other group in one of two ways:

(a) having worked cooperatively 'in-group' would encourage greater cooperation toward working with another group. In other words, there would be a 'carry-over effect': groups that had enjoyed working together cooperatively would go on to display the same style of working with other groups;

(b) that in-group cooperation would have the effect of increasing a group's sense of identity. A strong sense of identity would therefore strengthen the division between that group and other groups, and thus produce competitiveness when working with a different group. In-group cooperation would actively discourage cooperation with other groups rather than be carried over into working together.

Similarly they were interested in possible 'carry-over' effect from working competitively. They again envisaged two hypothetical results once groups that had worked competitively went to work with another group:

(a) that there would be a carry-over effect: in-group conflict would reproduce itself in competitiveness toward an out-group;

(b) that conflict within the group would mean that any group identity formed was not very strong and so working with another group might result in a less competitive approach. Group members might be relieved not to be put in a competitive situation and respond with cooperation.

In both cases – cooperative and competitive styles of working – the researchers conclude that their data supported the carry-over hypotheses. Groups that had worked cooperatively were cooperative again when subsequently working with another group. Groups that had experienced internal conflict were competitive with other groups, although this carry-over effect was less marked than the carry-over effect of being cooperative.

The implications of such research indicate that grouping practices in classrooms are not 'neutral' in terms of what children are learning over and beyond the direct object of the lesson. We must be careful not to adopt practices that might look to improve the mathematical learning if the cost of these is to limit the development of classroom community, and possibly life beyond the classroom.

Group composition

Young learners of mathematics are taught within a particular culture of mathematics that is inextricably linked to the prevailing culture of the community and the commonly held views of what it is to learn mathematics and who can succeed at it. The communities that we inhabit (in England certainly, but also elsewhere) do transmit, tacitly, values about learning mathematics and these often take the form either of 'not everyone can do maths' or 'it's not worth the effort'. Both of these views are not tenable and need challenging. International studies show that learning mathematics need not be like this. In Pacific Rim countries such as China or Japan the levels of understanding are much higher, especially at primary school, across nearly all children. Now it may be that children in Japan have to pay a price for success in mathematics (Leung 2002) but it does show that the commonly held view that only some children can 'get' maths is not the case.

I don't wish to be overly deterministic here in suggesting that culture is the dominant factor in learning. Clearly there are differences in opinion within the culture over how mathematics is taught and learned. A notable example is the continuing debate over whether or not children should be put into ability groups for learning maths – there is no universal agreement here. But I do suggest that there is an overriding cultural belief that is more dominant than others over the idea that there is a natural variation to the 'amount' of mathematics that young learners can 'acquire' (based in common metaphors of the brain as container and some brains having more 'capacity' for mathematics than others). As I argued earlier, this is based on the child at the center of learning. Thinking about learning as taking part in activities that themselves are located within communities requires us to look at the whole picture of why some children succeed and others do not, rather than focus on the individual as the main cause of difference. Bruner examines the importance and power of moving to focus on 'communities of learners':

> Indeed, on the basis of what we have learned in recent years about human learning – that it is best when it is participatory, proactive, communal, collaborative, and given over to constructing meanings rather than receiving them – we even do better at teaching science, maths, and languages in such schools than in more traditional ones.
> (Bruner 1996: 84)

Some findings from the Leverhulme Numeracy Research Programme at King's College, London, illustrate the importance of looking at activity systems rather than just elements within these. This five-year longitudinal study, directed by my colleague Margaret Brown, collected a wealth of data on teaching and learning in numeracy (the 'number' aspects of the curriculum) of four- to eleven-year-olds during the period 1997–2002. During that time England introduced its 'National Numeracy Strategy', one stated aim of which was to reduce the 'spread of attainment' between the highest and lowest attaining children in primary schools. Our data allowed us to compare classes of eight- and nine-year-olds before and after the introduction of the NNS. We assessed around 2,000 children of this age (Year 4) in 1997 – two years before the national adoption of the NNS. In the same schools we assessed the Year 4 classes again in 2002; these children had experienced two years of teaching based on the recommendations of the NNS. The spread of attainment for this latter group was actually marginally wider than for the historically older group. The higher attaining children (top 5 percent) performed at a slightly higher level than the equivalent group had done five years previously, while the performance of the bottom 5 percent was slightly worse than before (Brown, Askew *et al.* 2003). It is reasonable to assume that the intakes of the schools had not changed that much over the five years. It is the different histories of these children's learning that must have made the difference, not the children themselves and a key difference here was whether or not teaching had followed the model of the 'three-part-lesson' and framework of detailed objectives. Our observations of lessons in the schools pre and post the introduction of the National Numeracy Strategy supported this conjecture (Millett, Askew *et al.* 2004). Lessons were more constrained in 2002 than in 1997, together with more evidence of grouping children by 'ability'. As Robin Alexander notes, we must be careful that our practices do not cause children to 'drift apart and having so drifted [be] forced further apart by differential treatment' (Alexander 2010: 379).

Strength in diversity

Of course this is not to deny that children learn at different rates. Put a group of toddlers together in the same room and they will not all demonstrate the same levels of competency in walking. But they do all get there eventually (physical handicaps aside). A class of 30 ten-year-olds will be at different levels of mathematical attainment and for the teacher, having a group of children to teach where the spread of attainment is less extreme may make life easier. But we must be clear about for whose benefit setting children may work – it's mainly for the teachers' benefit. We may claim it is also for the learners' benefit but the research actually shows otherwise.

For example, Good and Brophy have extensively reviewed the literature on grouping pupils by ability (1997) and conclude that, at best, the higher attaining pupils may achieve a little more when they are taught as a separate group, but the gains here are not huge. And the cost to this is that over time the gap between higher and lower attaining children does widen. There is considerable evidence that children in lower sets quickly come to see themselves as not as good at maths and those in higher sets (actually the top set) as being 'best' and so live up or down to these self-attributions. As Robin Alexander and his colleagues note:

> [T]he evidence suggests there are no consistent effects of structured ability grouping, such as setting, on attainment, although there can be detrimental affects [sic] on social and personal outcomes for some children. Teaching quality seems to be the most important factor in determining outcomes, although pupils in the top groups can have an enhanced educational experience.
>
> (Alexander 2010: 290)

I've often presented teachers with these results and have been challenged with comments like 'well in our school, we have gone over to setting and results have gone up' but when pressed there are conflating factors at play that could equally account for gains. For example, many schools in setting for mathematics manage teaching resources in ways that allow for smaller classes – this could be what accounts for the rise in scores rather than the setting itself.

Getting tied up in knots over whether or not to set or put children into ability groups is predicated on an (usually unquestioned) assumption that diversity of understanding in the mathematics classroom is a 'problem' that needs to be 'minimized' or 'managed'. Reframing the issue dissolves the problem. Lo Mun Ling and colleagues, for example, argue that individual differences should not be used as an excuse for children not learning the intended curriculum.

> Therefore, in catering for individual differences, our focus is not on the variation in abilities; rather, we focus on the variation in learning outcomes. We believe that, if we can help students at acquire more powerful ways of seeing, it will be more likely that they are able to achieve the intended learning outcomes.
>
> (Lo, Pong and Chik 2005: 13)

In other words, rather than seeing individual differences as an 'input' variable that somehow has to be managed and reduced, we could shift our attention to the 'output' and accept that there will be a variety of learning outcomes (which is the case even in carefully setting classes).

Another way to reframe the issue of 'ability' is to see diversity in classrooms as an asset. The education system, and school in particular, is one of the few places where it is assumed that learning best flourishes by being grouped with others of 'like' ability (or age). But look at children's worlds. They are filled with parents, grandparents, older and younger siblings, 'aunts and uncles' and a myriad of relationships hardly any of which are with people of 'matched' ability and children learn a huge amount in their worlds. Narrow, skills-based learning might be best learned in narrow, ability-based groups, but only a small part of the mathematics curriculum is now focused on narrow skills acquisition. Given that it looks unlikely in the short term that schools will be reorganized along lines that are not arranged by age, we can make better use of the diversity within classrooms, rather than trying to reduce it. If, through the lens of complexity theory, our gaze is on the collective as well as the individual, then for emergent collective intelligent activity, such as unscripted cooperative problem solving, diversity is essential: 'A critical point here is that one cannot specify in advance what sorts of variation will be necessary for appropriately intelligent action, hence the need to ensure and maintain diversity in the current system' (Davis and Sumara 2006: 138).

Characteristics of effective creative groups

Keith Sawyer (2007) has studied how ideas emerge from group activity and strongly argues that creativity is collaborative and not the outcome of individual activity. Although Sawyer's main sites of study are organizations and corporations that have effective creative teams, I think some of the key characteristics that he identifies (pp. 14–17) can be adapted and applied to fostering creative mathematical classroom communities.

Learning emerges over time

I've discussed how we need to move away from thinking of the 'lesson' as the unit in which learning occurs and need to acknowledge that learning, in the sense of understanding and meaning in mathematics, emerges over time. Think about, say, coming to understand multiplication – this is not an all or nothing or quick process. We might even ask whether we ever come to the end of understanding. I'm often reading new research into aspects of mathematics that challenge my belief that I've come to understand everything there is about teaching or learning multiplication. Things like the demand for lessons to have 'pace' must not result in trying to rush through activity or replacing mathematical activity with actions. Aside from not acknowledging the need for time in learning, too much attention to pace may actually diminish learning: studies have shown that the application of time pressure can reduce learning (Lerch, Gonzalez *et al.* 1999).

Successful collaborative classrooms practice deep listening

We have a lot of talk and attention to speaking and listening, and while many classrooms have gone a long way to improving children's speaking in mathematics lessons, I think we still have a way to go in promoting deep listening.

As teachers we need to practice this and it is easier said than done. You go into a lesson with an idea of what you want to teach and it's hard not to be filtering out things that do not fit. This is not a criticism of teachers but actually a natural part of the way that the mind works. Classrooms bombard teachers with so much information.

As I argued in Chapter 4, actors trained in improvisation practice deep listening.

But we also need to encourage children to listen more closely to each other's mathematical ideas, and part of that comes from the next characteristic. I return to look at this in practice in Chapter 10.

Class members build on each other's ideas

Often, 'sharing' at the end of mathematics lessons does not have this vital component of ideas and solutions being built upon. What you get are a series of monologues – children coming up to present 'their' ideas (that is, an idea owned by the individual child rather than something being offered for shared ownership by the class, something to build on).

The work of Cathy Fosnot with Marteen Dolk and their 'Young Mathematicians at Work' (YMW) materials provide wonderful examples of children practicing deep listening and building on each other's ideas (see, for example, Fosnot and Dolk 2001a, b). Working on problems over several days the children collaborate initially in pairs to find a solution. While they are doing this the teacher is looking for solutions to be shared with the class that have the potential to build and develop the collective mathematical understanding. From the outside this can look like the more usual practice of sharing and celebrating a range of solutions that children have created. But there are subtle differences. In particular, the teacher does not ask for volunteers to share as that may not produce the solutions that will be of most benefit to everyone. Nor does she seek out the most unusual or novel or even most efficient solution method. The choice of solutions to be shared is mindfully selected by the teacher to maximize the likelihood that collective mathematical meaning can emerge. A further advantage of selecting who is going to share in advance is for the children to think about and rehearse what they are going to say to the class. Also, the children listening and not caught up in wondering whether they are going to be called upon next and paying more attention to mentally rehearsing their 'spot' than listening to what is being offered. Thus, the quality of both the speaking and listening is improved which in turn makes the collective discussion richer. (Of course, over time, we need to ensure that all the children get the opportunity to explain.)

Meaning becomes clear at the end

I wrote earlier of one of the YMW problems about division in the context of drinks machines. The teacher here did not start the lesson by saying 'today we are learning about division'. The formal mathematical models of the problems, in the form of division 'sentences', were only introduced during the plenary discussion of the solution. The formal mathematical sentences thus provided a means of linking together the different informal solutions that the children had come up with and helped the collective realize how these can be reinterpreted, and applied to other contexts. The meaning of the mathematical symbols thus becomes clear at the end of solving the problem, rather than being an 'input' at the beginning. As Bernie Neville notes, although it might appear more efficient to set things up at the beginning, explanations are actually more effective when children have had the experience to which they can be applied:

> Verbal instruction is productive if it comes after indirect learning: to clarify, to answer questions, to provide labels for the ideas that have arisen. In other words, it is effective in teaching what is already known but not adequately verbalized. Instruction directed at complete ignorance and disinterest raises no ripples at all. It is certainly not time-effective.
>
> (Neville 2005)

Meaning emerges from the bottom up

The examples that I have presented earlier I hope demonstrate this. The understanding of place value, or of how to add several two-digit numbers, emerges bottom-up from the activity of pairs of children and through sharing the results of that activity collective understanding can emerge. This is in contrast to starting with a neatly 'packaged' idea, carefully explaining it and hoping that the learners will accept this. This may look more efficient, but if we want mathematics learning to be meaningful and mindful then we need to build up from what the learners know and can do.

To sum up, the emergence of meaning is a collective endeavor rather than an individual one. The individual learning and meaning-making is a consequence of being part of a community that is striving toward reaching a collective understanding, through joint activity, dialogue.

Summary

Creating the sort of communities that I am arguing for here is not a case of simply saying to children, 'OK, let's work together now.' There has to be some sharing of values in ways that allow for diversity. 'As social beings, we are products of as well as contributors to traditions of behavior. We are not first disengaged, rational mechanisms, and *then* participants in a society' (Noddings 2002: 62, original emphasis).

This draws our attention to two points. First, as I have been arguing, views of whether or not children can all attain a reasonably high level of mathematics, especially in primary schools, is as much, if not mainly, a matter of cultural beliefs and tradition as the result of hard facts about the mathematical brain.

Second, as teachers we are born into and educated into a particular set of beliefs and become contributors to these – by accepting without question practices such as setting for mathematics we are tacitly agreeing with the view that different children have different mathematical capacities and so our practices continue to reinforce the apparent 'truths' rather than test and challenge them.

Mathematics can provide a strong forum for shared values within diversity. Moving to mathematics-centered classrooms, as opposed to pupil-centered or teacher-centered, means taking the diversity of the approaches and methods developed and exploring these in terms of the mathematics (as opposed to the 'smartness' or 'correctness' of the individuals proposing the solutions). Shared values around the ideas of what makes for a good mathematical argument or solution can help learners develop as a community as well as mathematically.

Further reading

Building Community in Schools by Thomas J. Sergiovanni. Sergiovanni has written many books and articles on school leadership but I particularly recommend this one. Here I have drawn upon the parts of this book that look at the importance of community building within classrooms, but the book goes beyond this and argues for the importance of community building within the staff of schools. The book is a rich blend of the theoretical and the practical.

Group Genius: the Creative Power of Collaboration by Keith Sawyer. Sawyer has studied jazz and improvisational drama groups and is interested in creativity. Like Sir Ken Robinson, the British writer and speaker on creativity, Sawyer is keen to dismiss the idea that being creative is something only some people can or do engage in. In this book he looks at the evidence for why group collaboration can help everyone be more creative.

Part 3

Teaching tripod

Chapter 9

Tasks

> Mathematics educators often cannot identify key mathematical understandings by examining their own mathematical understandings. What were key developmental issues early in the development of their understandings are not apparent as they now look at and through their sophisticated understandings. Indeed, many key understandings develop without students' awareness that a conceptual advance has taken place.
>
> (Simon 2006)

In this final third of the book I move to more specifically practical considerations based around a model of three aspects that need to be considered when planning for communities of mathematicians. I call these the 'teaching tripod':

- Tasks
- Tools
- Talk.

There is something powerful and appealing about metaphors where things come in threes: three bears, three wise men, three coins in a fountain. When it comes to legs, tripods are particularly stable – two-legged tables won't stand up on their own and four-legged tables can easily develop a 'wobble' on an uneven surface. Tripods stand steady.

I have argued that teaching mathematics requires a careful blend or preparation and improvisation. One of the points I made earlier is that trying to plan the content of a lesson too closely can close things down and lead to limited opportunities for learning. On the other hand simply going into a lesson with an open book and expecting the classroom mathematicians to spontaneously emerge is equally unhelpful. I suggest that the teaching tripod can maximize the likelihood of mathematics emerging from lessons. By attending to each of the elements in the teaching tripod lessons can be structured to be sufficiently open to allow children to bring their mathematical knowledge to bear, but also sufficiently structured to allow some degree of control over the direction of the mathematics.

In this chapter I look at the first 'leg' of the teaching tripod: tasks. Tasks – what teachers ask children to engage with – are central to mathematics lessons. Tasks embody, often implicitly, our views on the relationship between teaching and learning. One goal of this chapter is to make some of these views more explicit, so that we can be more considered in our choice of tasks. The second goal of the chapter is to examine the relationship between tasks and the subsequent mathematical activity that children engage in. On the basis of this I argue for mathematical activity to be focused around problem solving and look at how this might be put into practice. The following chapters look in turn at tools and talk.

Task and activity

We need to distinguish between tasks – what teachers set for children to do – and the subsequent mathematical activity that children, collectively, engage in to carry out the task. If children are going to develop mathematical confidence, curiosity and a have-a-go attitude there needs to be a certain 'gap' between the task that a teacher sets and the children's subsequent mathematical activity. Teaching which strives to narrow the gap between task and activity, for example through careful instructions that children have to follow, may lead to short-term success but not long-term learning.

I explore this task–activity gap in two parts. First I look at one of the commonly embedded metaphors that we use to talk about learning: the metaphor of 'seeing'. Through the example of 'recognizing' fractions I demonstrate that this is far from being a simple process of perception and that identifying fractions is a complex problem-solving activity in which children not so much recognize but actively re-cognize. Following that I look at some of the sorts of tasks that can provide this critical gap between task and activity, particularly problem-solving tasks.

I use learning about fractions as an example throughout this chapter. While this will provide insight into issues about teaching fractions, I suggest that these issues are not limited only to understanding fractions but apply to the majority of mathematics. Through these examples, I hope to show that less of learning mathematics is procedural than we might think. Even something that appears as straightforward and based on fluency as recognizing simple fractions such as halves or quarters is deeply embedded in a network of mathematical activity.

Recognize or re-cognize?

The processes of being socialized into the activity of reading fraction diagrams are largely hidden from us. Not only do simple fractions appear somewhat obvious to adults, fraction diagrams are presented in ways that remove ambiguity and learners are rarely asked about the variety of possible interpretations. Indeed, when learners produce an alternative 'reading' of a mathematical image, we tend to talk of these as being 'misconceptions', 'bugs' in the learners' thinking, rather like 'bugs' in a computer program, that need fixing. Rather than treat alternative readings as errors, as something to be erased, corrected or prevented from arising in the first place, Langer's research on being mindful suggests that these could be a valuable source of dialogue and the perfect opportunity to explore the conditionality of mathematics ideas (Langer 1989).

> In most educational settings, the 'facts' of the world are presented as unconditional truths, when they might be better in some contexts but not in others. What happens when this uncertainty is allowed in? Does the uncertain information become more available to use later, when the context has changed?
>
> (Langer 1989: 120)

Langer's research leads her to answer 'yes' to this last question. Consider this example. The 'typical' response to asking what fraction the shaded part in Figure 9.1 represents is ¼.

The answer ¼ is not a fixed property of the diagram but conditional upon the implicit agreement that what is being asked for is a comparison of the part to the whole. Compare that with your response to this question:

Are there more women in the country, or people?

Bit of a stupid question. Posing this question out loud and emphasizing the pause marked by the comma sets up an expectation that the end of the question will be 'or men'. What's the point of comparing women to people? In our everyday lives, we don't go around comparing part of the group to the whole group; not only is the answer obvious, but it does not lead to any new insight. Piaget, in a classic research, demonstrated how children found it difficult to answer questions where they needed to compare part of the collection to all of it. For example, given a bunch of red and white roses, with more red than white, and asked, 'Are there more red roses or roses?' young children would answer, 'red'. Although subsequent research has indicated that children's success rates can be improved by putting the question into a somewhat more realistic context (such as comparing cows sleeping in a field to the herd of cows), the point nevertheless remains. It is rare to find ourselves needing to compare part of a collection to the whole thing.

But that is what we implicitly do when interpreting Figure 9.1 as ¼. The comparison is between the number of shaded parts, one, to the total number of parts, four, including the shaded part itself (women to people!). If, more often than not, we compare part-to-part, then it is likely that children will bring this everyday expectation of comparing to bear when dealing with fractions. The children's strategies and mathematics and science research (Hart 1981) did indeed show that when asked what fraction Figure 9.1 represented a substantial proportion of 14-year-olds gave the answer one third: a part-to-part comparison interpretation of the question. A perfectly sensible interpretation, and one which in other wordings of the question would be the correct answer (these are black and white counters, what is the ratio of black counters to white counters?).

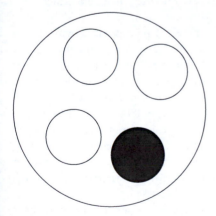

Figure 9.1 What fraction is shaded?

It is possible to imagine a world of mathematics where the answer to 'what fraction does Figure 9.1 represent?' is indeed 'one third': fractions as a result of comparing part-to-part. Understanding fractions, and most other aspects of mathematics, is not simply a matter of frequent exposure and the subsequent ability to 'recognize' something.

Research carried out by Marty Simon and colleagues demonstrated the prevalence of teachers talking about learning mathematics in terms of a perceptual process, particularly reliant on sight.

> Our claim is that the teachers participated in educational situations as if the mathematical relationships that are (or can be) perceived were properties of the objects being considered (e.g., base-ten blocks), not a function of the knowledge of the perceiver . . . We describe the teachers in this group as having a perception-based perspective that includes the perspectives on mathematics and mathematical understanding just described but that also takes as essential for learning (with understanding) the learner's direct personal perception of mathematical relationships. That is, for learners to attain the intended quality of learning (understanding), they must 'see' for themselves the mathematical relationships that exist among mathematical entities.
>
> (Simon, Tzur *et al.* 2000: 592–3)

So ingrained is this sight metaphor that it is taken for granted in defining learning outcomes. For example, England's national numeracy framework specified children 'recognizing' fractions. The case study of Meg demonstrates how the metaphor of recognizing breaks down when even a small change is made to what has been seen before.

I think Meg was acting in a highly mathematical fashion in addressing her difficulty. She was not just mindlessly trying to guess the answer to the question; she was mindfully thinking about the possible interpretations of the diagram and trying to come to a general conclusion. No amount of sitting and staring at the diagram and thinking about the range of possible interpretations would have led to Meg being able to decide for herself what was the accepted answer. There also needs to be discussion within the classroom community on different interpretations and which one has been agreed on. Developing mathematical understanding is not an individual, isolated, activity; it is embedded in a collective activity.

Coming to 'see' fractions within diagrams is not merely a perceptual activity, not a case of recognizing, but a cognitive activity, a process of re-cognizing. And this is not a solitary cognitive action; it arises out of a stream (historical) of social and cultural mathematical activity. The 'knowledge' of fractions is not something 'out there' that has to be 'delivered' and which children somehow have to 'internalize'. Young learners, in a real sense, have to go through what 'mathematics' learnt about fractions, although in a much shorter time-scale. Rather than trying to sidestep this complexity we need to engage children in mathematical activity rather than assume that knowledge is something that they lack, we have and simply need to pass on to them. We have to help children become knowing, through collective activity, rather than see them as passive recipients of knowledge.

As Davis and Sumara point out, our everyday language is peppered with metaphors that suggest a separation of knowledge from knowers: we scaffold learning, 'see' what

Meg

Meg, aged seven, was doing some introductory work on fractions. Working from a textbook, the instruction was to decide whether each diagram on the page showed ½, ¼ or ⅛. Most of the diagrams were typical of this sort of exercise and Meg had correctly written down the accepted answer for the first few diagrams, which were similar to those in Figure 9.2.

However, toward the bottom of the page was a less obvious diagram (Figure 9.3). Meg was looking puzzled.

'Are you okay?' I asked.

'No,' replied Meg, 'I'm stuck on this one.'

'Why?'

'Well, I think it could be any of these. You see a half (pointing to the symbol ½ at the top of the page) has a two in it, and there are two pieces shaded here. Or it could be a quarter, 'cos there are four pieces here (tracing out the right-hand side of the diagram with her finger) and they've shaded in one of them (pointing to the bottom shaded piece). I don't know why, but they've done it twice (indicating the left-hand side diagram). Or it could be an eighth, because there are eight pieces and one of these (pointing to one of the shaped pieces) would be an eighth. And they've done it twice.'

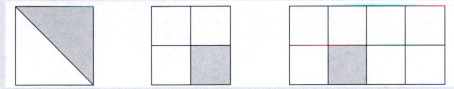

Figure 9.2 What fraction – ½, ¼ or ⅛?

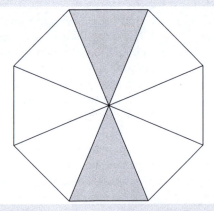

Figure 9.3 A less obvious fraction

someone is 'getting at' or have difficulty 'getting our heads round' something. The difficulty with this, they argue, is that it perpetuates the view that

> knowers and knowledge are discontinuous. They have most often been cast in terms of two separate domains that must somehow be bridged . . . The assumption of such a gap is particularly troublesome for educators, who, within such a frame, are assumed to straddle the two realms. The role of educators is thus typically described in terms of the dual responsibility of representing objective knowledge and fostering subjective knowledge, but these roles are usually understood as existing in tension.
>
> (Davis and Sumara 2006: 154)

I am suggesting that this tension can be reduced through collective engagement in mathematical activity generating improvised solutions that can be discussed and mathematized. Generating improvised solutions means starting with a problem-solving context that is meaningful to children. If they cannot 'buy into' the problem then they are not going to be able to generate solutions. The 'Pizzas' example illustrates this and comes from a lesson with nine-year-olds. The children were having difficulties with fractions and with the idea of equivalence in particular. So we, the teacher and I, planned a lesson around an everyday situation that we thought the children would understand: sharing pizzas.

Pizzas

We spent a lot of time at the beginning of the lesson talking about the context – going out with friends or family for a pizza – in general and not rushing to introduce the actual problem, setting up an atmosphere in the classroom that says 'we', the teachers, are interested in what 'you', the children, are bringing to the problem (in this case, about fair shares).

Finally we posed the problem, verbally:

12 friends went out for a pizza. It was toward the end of the month, so they only had enough money to order 8 pizzas. They ordered the 8 and shared them equally. How much pizza did each person get?

The children cooperated in small groups, recording on one large piece of paper and with a single thick marker pen. While they figured out solutions we went round encouraging the children to explain their methods. As things were drawing to a conclusion we selected two solutions that we thought should be shared with the class and told the children in those groups to be prepared to come up and address the class.

The first method (Figure 9.4) was typical of what many groups had done: everyone got half a pizza each and the remaining two pizzas could be sliced into sixths. So the friends got ½ + ⅙ pizza each.

The other solution was based on sharing four pizzas so that everyone would get ⅓ pizza (Figure 9.5). The second four pizzas would provide another ⅓ each. So in this group each person would get ⅔ of a pizza. (Figure 9.5 shows that some work needed to done later on in helping the children represent thirds as equal-sized pieces, but the principle of their argument was correct.)

The formalizing part of this lesson came at the end when the two solutions to be presented were chosen because the mathematics looked different.

After both solutions had been presented and discussed, the class was in agreement that each was correct. But what was happening here? Going out with one group could mean getting ½ + ⅙ of a pizza to eat, going with the other group could give you ⅔ pizza. Were these the same? If you really liked pizza which group would you want to go out with?

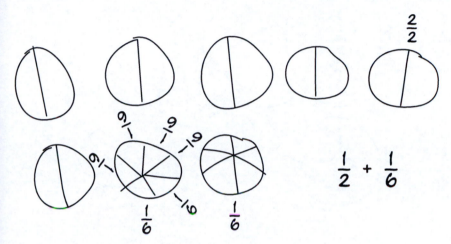

Figure 9.4 Solution to the pizza problem 1

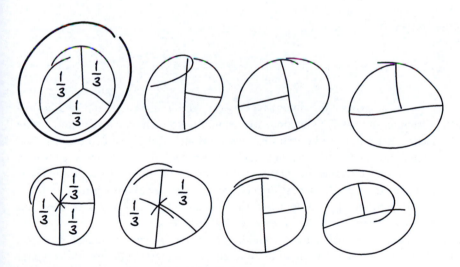

Figure 9.5 Solution to the pizza problem 2

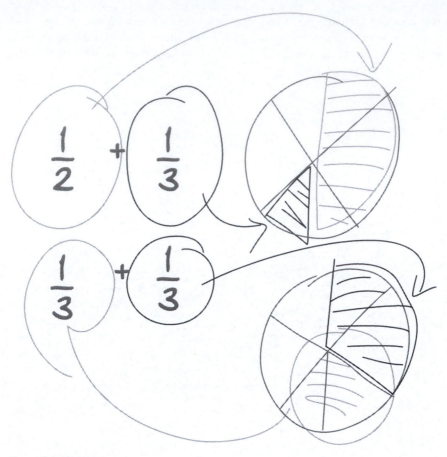

Figure 9.6 Equivalence

This is a point at which the interplay between the improvised and the formal mathematics becomes crucial. The children were mindful from their everyday knowledge that, if the sharing had been fair in each case, the portions would have to be equal. The challenge was to sort out why, mathematically, these two solutions appeared to be different. This is a key difference in *starting* with a problem. Improvised knowledge is used to support emergent mathematical understanding. This stands in contrast with the teach-the-content-first-then-apply-it approach that assumes children can easily access and use abstract mathematics to make sense of everyday situations.

Back in their groups we challenged the children to come up with some representation that would show whether the two amounts were equal or different. Figure 9.6 is typical of the diagrams they produced to show equality. The plenary discussion about what they'd learnt indicated that many of the children were beginning to get a sense of what equivalence was really about.

Realistic mathematics education

The Realistic Mathematics Education curriculum developed in Holland is based around this idea of 'mathematizing' from problems that children can initially solve informally. The Dutch researchers draw attention to two different sorts of mathematizing. Horizontal mathematizing, they argue, is the process of moving from a realistic situation to the setting up of a mathematical model. In the case of the pizza problem the initial diagrams that the children produced are examples of horizontal mathematizing.

Vertical mathematizing, according to the Dutch work, is the activity of moving between different mathematical models. When we challenged the children to sort out whether the two different solutions did produce the same amount of pizza, then the diagrams they produced were more aligned to thinking about two different mathematical models and so the children were beginning to engage in vertical mathematizing (although there are still echoes of the pizzas in their work).

When planning and selecting problems it pays to think through what the children's initial models, usually in the form of diagrams, might look like. In this particular example the choice of fractions that we were working with did lend itself to a circular representation and so pizzas were an obvious choice for the real-world context. Had we chosen, say, chocolate to share instead, then the children would have been more likely to set up representations that were rectangular images, which may then have been easier to divide up into twelve 'chunks' and so a different set of representations to work with would have emerged. That is not to say that chocolate bars would have been better or worse, but the subsequent improvised solutions and mathematical conversation would have been different.

Problem-solving pedagogy

In this section I further elaborate how problem solving can provide a starting point from which to build mathematical understanding rather than the endpoint of mathematical application. Working with problems as vehicles for learning requires a style of teaching that begins with engaging the children with the problem. We need to be providers of mathematical tasks that are likely to lead to rich mathematical activity. Some writers prefer to talk about 'rich mathematical tasks'. I am not convinced by calling a task rich (with the metaphoric overtones of a cake being 'rich' because of the amount of butter it contains). There is a danger that talk of rich tasks is interpreted as tasks having to be elaborate or complicated. The problems the children described here were relatively simple problems; the richness rests in the activity that emerged by encouraging them to take a creative stance to solving the problems.

If children are to learn from their problem-solving experiences then the problems have to be chosen in the expectation that children will need to sustain activity on them for some time. We need to question the popularly held view that 'speed' is a key marker of mathematical ability. While there is some advantage to being able to rapidly recall addition and multiplication bonds, problem solving requires a different style of thinking, one that involves mulling and puzzling and chewing things over rather than rushing and competing and acting mindlessly. Learners have to be able to tolerate a certain amount of ambiguity when thinking about and solving problems, which is different from the sort of precision that is needed in finding exact answers to calculation.

The children's improvised solutions to problems are not the end of the story, but only the beginning of the development of the formal mathematics. An important, if not the important, part of the lesson is the drawing together of strands of mathematics from the various solutions the children offer. As indicated in the pizza problem a class dialogue has to have a clear mathematical focus. Coming together to look at solutions is not simply a time for celebrating the inventiveness or variety of children's solutions. A crucial role of the teacher is to decide which of the children's improvised solutions will provide the opportunity for rich dialogue with the class about the mathematics. The solutions to the pizza problem were chosen in the expectation that they might provoke some mindful 'cognitive conflict' in the children – by appearing to be very mathematically different, how could this fit in with children's everyday understanding of sharing out pizzas? It is not just a question of asking the volunteers at the end of the lesson. Nor is it simply a matter of choosing the children with the most sophisticated solution – it may well be that such a solution may be too far removed from what the other children's solutions have done to be up to making sense of it, and adjust their thinking about their own solutions in the light of the dialogue.

Opening up the gap between task and activity

What then are some ways of turning usual tasks into ones with potential for rich mathematical activities?

Over the years, I have found Marion Walter and Stephen Brown's work to be invaluable in developing rich mathematical activities (Brown and Walter 1990). The basic tenet of their work is to list the elements of a problem (including rather obvious ones) and from this list of 'what is' ask 'what if not': how changing some of the givens might lead to further mathematical activity.

For example, a simple question is $25 + 25 = 50$

What is	What if not
25 and 25	Other doubles, for example, 36 and 36
	Other multiples of 5, for example 25 and 45
Two numbers added	What sets of three numbers add to 50?
	Sets of four numbers?
Adding to 50	What other pairs of numbers add to 50?
	What pairs of numbers have a difference of 50?
	What pairs of numbers have a product of 50?
	What pairs of numbers divide to give 50?
Both less than 50	Can you have a pair of numbers that add to 50 where one of the numbers is bigger than 50?
Whole numbers	What if we include fractions?

Not all of the resulting questions are equally curious, but some may be worth pursuing. Playing around with doubling multiples of three can lead to insights into the relationship between multiples of three and multiples of six for example.

Here are some examples of the what-if-not technique in practice. I am grateful to Ann Watson and John Mason for drawing my attention to the power of asking for at least three examples (Watson and Mason 2005). When asked to create something the first one or even two examples are usually quite straightforward. It's when you get up to three that the interesting stuff starts to happen. I find this also works with posing problems – using this technique to create one or two new problems is usually quite easy. It is when you get to thinking up the third problem that it starts to get challenging. I created the problems below using this rule of three and present them in the order in which they were created – you may like to consider how you think the third problem compares to the first two.

CLOSED TASK

$3 \times 4 =$

Invitation to mathematical activity

- What if not multiplication?
    How many different numbers can you make by combining 3 and 4 using any operations?
- What if not find the product?
    Can you find at least three multiplication calculations with 12 as the answer?
- What if not the product of two numbers?
    Can you find 3 numbers that multiplied together have a product of 12? Four numbers? . . .

CLOSED TASK

What is the area and perimeter of the shape in Figure 9.7?

Invitation to mathematical activity

- What if not find the area?
    Can you draw at least three shapes with the same area as the one below, but with a different perimeter?
- What if not find the perimeter?

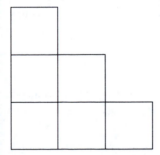

Figure 9.7 Area and perimeter

> Can you draw at least three shapes with the same perimeter, but with a different area?

- What if not squares?

> Draw a shape with six equilateral triangles. Investigate what happens to the perimeter of the shape if you rearrange the triangles.

CLOSED TASK

If a chocolate bar costs 38p, how much change would you get from 50p?

Invitation to mathematical activity

- What if not change?

> How many ways can you find to pay 38p exactly?

- What if not cost?

> I went out shopping, handed over a single coin, and got 12p change. How much might the things I bought have cost?

- What if not 38p?

> I found four coins down the back of the sofa. What different amounts could I pay exactly and not require any change?

Summary

I have argued that learning mathematics which is not based on procedural fluency but which involves understanding means learners are active constructors of knowledge, not passive recipients of it. Teaching must use and build on children's active sense making. With this, has to be the acceptance that, in the early stages of mathematical activity, there will be a certain amount of messiness as ideas emerge, are refined and made formal. Rather than try and avoid this messiness through careful and unambiguous explanations or demonstrations at the beginning of a lesson, setting up tasks for the children to work on with a certain amount of uncertainty in how they have to go about the task is a way to make them engage mindfully and bring their sense making to the activity.

Perfect for creating a task/activity gap are problems which require learners to produce improvised solutions – that is, solutions that are worked out in the moment, rather than pre-scripted (or even prescribed in the sense of only one solution method being acceptable).

Mathematical activity, just like physical activity, is enhanced by the judicious use of tools. In the next chapter I look at the sort of mental tools that we might help children develop the use of in support of their mathematical activity.

Further reading

The Art of Problem Solving by Stephen Brown and Marion Walter. A classic of mathematics education, full of examples illustrating how to create problems that are likely to lead to rich mathematical activity.

Mathematics as a Constructive Activity by Ann Watson and John Mason. Most of the examples are geared toward secondary mathematics but this is still a wealth of ideas that can be adapted to the primary classroom.

Chapter 10

Tools

> In short, because what we call mind works through artifacts, it cannot be uncondition-
> ally bounded by the head or even by the body, but must be seen as distributed in
> the artifacts which are *woven together* and which weave together individual human
> actions in concert with and as a part of the permeable, changing, events of life.
>
> (Cole 1996, original emphasis)

While there is general agreement about the importance of 'models and images' in helping
children learn mathematics, there is less clarity about why they are important and how
to work with them. It is not the models or images themselves that are important, but
the way that these support children's mathematical activity. Models and images have to
be worked with, not simply presented to the children. My preference is to talk about
tools, as tools are only useful when someone is using them. Images are often interpreted
as being self-evident. Models are a step on the road to tool use.

We are better off introducing children to a small number of models and working
intensively with these over time. Teaching is not insulated from the pressures to consume
and schools are inundated with catalogues of the latest posters, bricks, plastic bananas
or whatever we are told promise to help the children understand place value, or fractions
or fruit. Most of these are designed from the point of view of attractiveness rather than
pedagogical soundness. There is an assumption that presenting the base-ten structures
as, say, ten petals on a daisy, children will find these enticing, will want to work with
them and the mathematics will take care of itself. In my experience most of these colorful
manipulables are not that effective as models supporting mathematical activity. Similarly,
much of what gets presented on interactive whiteboards misses the mark – images that
are lively, enticing and that move can help children engage with the mathematics but
most of the time what attracts the children's attention is the nature of the images
themselves and they may not 'see through' these to encounter some mathematics. In
variation theory terms too much variation in the images may mask the mathematically
critical aspects and children's attention may be drawn to discerning variation amongst
the images rather than the mathematics.

My advice about models is that simpler is better. Were I teaching again I would equip
my class with base-ten blocks, interlocking cubes, a wide variety of 2D and 3D shapes
and lots of plain paper and colored pencils or pens. And that's about it.

Models, tools and artifacts

Let us return to Vygotsky (see Chapter 2), together with the research from the Freudenthal
Institute in Holland to use the term tool in a particular sense. Although many of Vygotsky's

observations about tool use still are pertinent today, recent research, particularly from neuroimaging, develops Vygotsky's ideas beyond what he could have theorized about (Carr 2010).

Vygotsky wrote about the distinction between physical tools and psychological tools (1978). Physical tools, he argued, are tools that extend our unaided capabilities and enable us to make changes to our environment that we would find difficult, if not impossible, without the tools. Typical are the tools such as we would find in any carpenter's toolbox or needleworker's sewing kit. Putting shelves up on the wall or embroidering a tablecloth both require the use of physical tools such as drills and spirit-levels or needles and scissors. Physical tools extend our 'natural' capabilities (natural in the sense of what we are capable of without the use of the tools).

Although physical tools extend our abilities and enable us to change the world around us, Vygotsky theorized that they were limited in the extent to which they change us as human beings. Physical tools, by and large, are designed for quite specific purposes and do not generalize in their application that easily. My hammer is not much use in my embroidery any more than my needle will help in putting up a cabinet. Similarly, a lot of hammering or fine sewing may improve some specific motor skills and hand–eye coordination, but these changes are mostly limited to these specific tool uses: the hand–eye coordination that I develop in learning to hammer accurately will not transfer to being able to embroider a delicate leaf, and vice versa.

The other type of tool – psychological tools – that Vygotsky identified not only allows us to change our environment but also has a profound effect back on us, on who we are, not simply what we can do. Language, Vygotsky argued, was the most powerful psychological tool. We tend not to talk about language as a tool, more often we think of language as labeling, describing our world. Young children take a delight in repeatedly asking 'what's that?' once they have a sense of language as a way of naming things, but language is not simply about labeling and naming. Vygotsky's argument was that we developed language as a tool to get things done. Names and labels, in and of themselves, are not important, but they enable us to accomplish things. 'Please pass the ketchup' is much easier than 'Please can you pass that thingy with the stuff the same color as that other thing I'm pointing to'. Just like physical tools, psychological tools enable action, but over and above that, they have a profound effect on who we are. The 'terrible twos' period of infancy has much to do with the child learning the power of the word 'no'! And the child who learns this is not the same child they were before.

Talk is such a powerful tool in learning and using mathematics, that rather than discuss it under this general heading of 'tools' I think it deserves attention in its own right and so it forms the third 'leg' of the teaching tripod and is the subject of the next chapter.

Mathematics is also a psychological tool; it not only enables us to achieve things that would be difficult, if not impossible, without it, but it also fundamentally transforms who we are. This can be a positive transformation if mathematics is taught in ways that acknowledge the 'human' side of the subject and that build on what learners can do and helps them to feel empowered.

Recent research into brain activity suggests that differences in the impact on us of physical and psychological tools may not be as great as Vygotsky theorized. For example, brain scans of monkeys that have been taught to use tools to get food that they cannot reach reveal that the 'brain maps' of the animals' hands actually changed: the tools were treated as being part of the hand, being incorporated into the brain's 'map' of the body. The monkeys' brains adapted as though the tool was a natural extension of their fingers (Marativa and

Iriki 2004). Studies on the human brain have found similar results. For example, it is now well established that learning to play the violin alters brain structure (Elbert, Pantev *et al.* 1995). In a way Vygotsky and Piaget were both right in a more profound sense than either could have anticipated. Vygotsky talked about 'internalization' as though the brain had to take external activity and transform it in some way to become something different and internal. Piaget used the ideas of accommodation and assimilation to account for how the brain adapted to external experiences. Both of these positions are based on a dualism, a split between the 'external world' and the mental 'internal world'. Brain research is suggesting that such dualism may be much less distinct. We may be 'embodied' and it may subjectively feel that as I hold my computer mouse that my hand is totally separate from the mouse, but as far as the brain is concerned, the sense of my skin marking the boundary between 'me' and the outside world is much less marked. I may be embodied but at a deep level the brain has evolved to allow the body to be extended. This has profound implications for the tools and artifacts that we present to children for learning mathematics. First, because the brain research shows that it takes time for the brain to adapt to specific tools: a brief introduction to number-lines or arrays in a particular year may not be enough for the learner to literally make these tools for thinking with. Second, we need to be sure that the models children experience are going to be of long-term benefit.

From models to tools

Tools are but 'artifacts' to the novice (Cole 1996); they start their psychological life as simply a physical presence but with no personal meaning. To a young child an analogue clock may make a good wheel, plate, or drum, but it is not a 'clock' to the child in the sense of something that we mark time with. The child is aware of the physical presence of artifacts, but not aware of their meaning in activity. Artifacts become tools when they come to serve the purpose and meaning with which experienced users imbue them. As teachers we introduce artifacts – and I am including marks on paper or the board here – that have meaning for us as teachers but have to come to be filled with meaning by the child. Such meaning cannot simply be explained; it comes about through joint activity. One of the challenges of teaching is trying to get back into that 'space' that learners occupy, as much of what we take for granted as 'meaningful' is not in and of itself full of meaning – it is the meaning that we bring to it.

This is also why mathematics starts to 'unravel' for so many learners with things like fractions or algebra; the symbols on the page stay at the level of 'artifacts', things that you manipulate with rules like 'turn it upside down and multiply' or 'move it to the other side of the equation and change the sign'. They are not meaning-filled by the learner.

We have to be careful about limiting the meaning that we allow symbols to become filled with, bringing us back to the importance of conditionality. If 'x' as in 3×4 is only ever made sense of as repeated addition then what can $\frac{1}{2} \times \frac{3}{4}$ possibly mean – how do we make sense of 'adding' a half three quarter times? Variety of mathematical activity promotes variety of meanings.

I am not restricting artifact to concrete 'manipulables' such as base-ten blocks or interlocking cubes, although I am including these. Pictures, diagrams, and, especially, mathematical symbols are only artifacts to the novice.

The work of the Dutch Realistic Mathematics Education at the Freudenthal Institute provides a framework for thinking about how we can help, and monitor, children moving from artifacts to tools. They distinguish between:

- models of
- models for
- tools for (Gravemeijer 1999).

Artifacts start life in the classroom as 'models of', in the sense that the teacher uses these with meaning and through joint activity the children begin to also 'read' meaning into the artifacts. To take a simple example, children will have informal strategies for solving addition problems in context. Adding four and three they may hold out four fingers and then another three and count the total. The teacher could provide a model of this by drawing a number line, counting along to four on the line and then counting on three more 'steps' to land on seven. This 'model of' the addition is not a transparent mirroring of what the children did: they were counting objects, the teacher is counting jumps.

Through the joint activity of the children solving the calculations in their own way and the teacher sharing her model of this then, over time, the children begin to appropriate the teacher's model and begin to use it for themselves: the number line has been transformed from a *model of* what the children did to a *model for* them to use themselves.

The Dutch research shows that over more time the children come to be able to work with the number line as a model for addition, but without needing to make actual marks on paper: it becomes a *tool for thinking* with.

There is a subtle distinction here between watching a lesson where a teacher models an addition on a number line: it can look as though the teacher is merely recording what the children are doing – she isn't – or using the number to 'explain' addition – it can't. The movement from a 'model of' to 'model for' to 'tool for thinking' takes time and children will not all move through these stages at the same rate.

I want to explore this further by contrasting the use of base-ten blocks for teaching subtraction compared to the empty number line. Although base-ten blocks might be good 'models of' subtraction, they can be problematic in terms of becoming 'models for' and even further removed from becoming tools for thinking.

Base-ten blocks, for any reader not familiar with them, are a set of wooden or plastic pieces that start with small 'ones' – 1-cm cubes. These are increasingly scaled up to provide a manipulative model of the base-ten system. There are 'longs' equivalent to ten 'ones' joined in a line; 'flats' equivalent to ten 'longs' in the form of a 10×10 square (1 cm deep); 'cubes' equivalent to ten 'flats' in a $10 \times 10 \times 10$ cube and thus equivalent to 1,000 'ones'. A number like 3,756 would be modeled with 3 'cubes', 7 'flats', 5 'longs' and 6 'ones'.

Typically, teachers would use these as a model of the operation of subtraction in anticipation of the decomposition algorithm. Something like 546 –289 would be modeled along the following lines. The 546 is set out with 5 flats, 4 longs and 6 ones. The task is to 'take-way' 289. Working from the units or ones in the right-hand column, the first step is to try and remove 9 unit cubes. As there are only 6 available, the teacher exchanges one of the 10 longs for 10 single ones. Now the 9 can be taken away from the 16 to leave 7 ones. There are now only 3 longs on the table: to take away the 80 we must exchange one of the 5 flats for 10 longs so there are now 4 flats and 13 longs. The 8 longs can be removed leaving 5 on the table and the 2 flats taken away from the 4 flats. So we are left with 2 flats, 5 longs and 7 ones, 257. These actions closely model the paper and pencil standard decomposition recording (Figure 10.1):

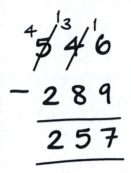

Figure 10.1 Decomposition

So far so good, the blocks do provide a perfectly good model of the decomposition algorithm when the actions with the blocks fit with the symbolic recording. Issues begin to arise when children subsequently use the blocks as models for doing subtraction by themselves. Note that there is nothing about the blocks in and of themselves that requires you to start with the ones – that's a convention as a result of the goal of the algorithm, not a necessary part of the activity. Assuming children do start with the units then, it is not very efficient when wanting to remove 9 ones to put a long back in the box, count out 10 individual ones and then count back 9 ones into the box. It is much simpler to put one long into the box and take back a single one, effectively 'taking away' the 9 in one move. Similarly the 5 tens can be taken away by putting one 'flat' back and bringing back 5 longs, rather than counting out 10 longs and then putting back 5. In other words the *models for* using these blocks that children develop are different from the *model of* that the teacher sets up.

Evidence now also shows that these 'blocks' do not easily lend themselves to becoming tools for thinking with. People's mental models of number seem to be linked to the ordinal aspects of number: where numbers are placed in order and with respect to each other, as on a linear scale or number line (Dehaene 1999). In other words, people's 'sense' of 546 is more closely linked to knowing it is between 500 and 600 and close to 550, than it is to picturing a pile of 550 individual items, even if these are organized as 5 lots of 100, 4 lots of 10 and 6 ones. Base-ten blocks present a different model, a cardinal one – what 546 looks like as a quantity in and of itself.

Let's compare this with modeling the subtraction on a number line. We would start with an empty number line with 546 marked toward the right-hand end of the line. Taking away is now modeled by jumping back 289 on the line. When you do this with children, they usually start by jumping back the largest amount, the 200 (Figure 10.2).

Then the 80 and then the 9 (Figure 10.3).

Like working with the blocks, the number line has the potential for other more efficient strategies to be explored. For example, noticing that 289 is not that far away from 300, we could subtract the 300 and then 'compensate' for the fact that we took away more than we needed to (Figure 10.4). Although this could have been done with base-ten blocks, it's clearer to see what is happening on the number line.

The model with the blocks was traditionally subtraction as 'taking away'; on the number line we can also model finding the difference. Now, rather than marking 546

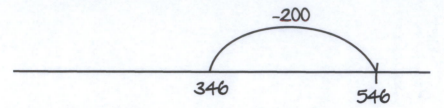

Figure 10.2 Taking away (1)

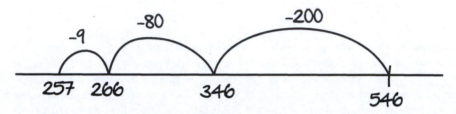

Figure 10.3 Taking away (2)

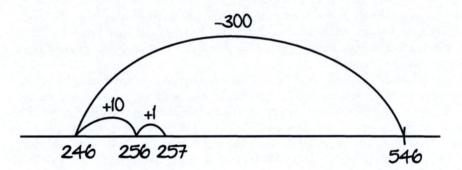

Figure 10.4 Compensation

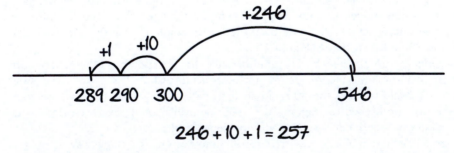

$$246 + 10 + 1 = 257$$

Figure 10.5 Finding the difference

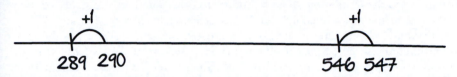

Figure 10.6 Constant difference (1)

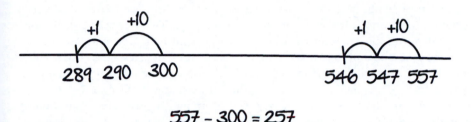

$$557 - 300 = 257$$

Figure 10.7 Constant difference (2)

and jumping back 289, we mark both numbers on the line and figure out the size of the difference between them. We can do this by counting up from the smaller number to the larger (Figure 10.5).

But again the number line lends itself to playing with the numbers. We might attend to the fact that 289 is close to 290, so if we add 1 to each number, the difference between them remains constant (constant difference – see Chapter 6 p. 68) (Figure 10.6).

We can make things even easier. Add another ten to each number (Figure 10.7).

Now all I have to do is find the difference between 300 and 557 – that's easy, 257. These models for carrying out subtraction on the number line do lend themselves to becoming tools for thinking with.

> '546 subtract 289. Well I can take away 300, that's 246 but that's 11 more than I need to take way, so eleven onto 246 is 257.'

Or

> '546 subtract 289. What's the difference between these two? Making 289 up to 300 means adding 11 to it. Adding 11 to 546 will preserve the difference. So that's 557. Difference between 557 and 300 is 257.'

If I get lost in the mental reasoning, a quick sketch can extend the mental screen. And I'm much more likely to have paper and pencil to hand than base-ten blocks. But there is more going on here, both in terms of variation and being mindful.

Examples and variation

An aspect of variation in these subtractions is the numbers, chosen to maximize the likelihood of children's awareness being drawn not only to the relationship between the two numbers but also to the relationship of each number to other numbers that could be used to make the calculation more 'friendly'. So 289 is deliberately close to 300 and 546 to 550. A calculation like 537 – 266 is less likely to provoke awareness of this possibility of using proximal numbers. Most pages of subtraction exercise in textbooks would not make any such distinction: practicing subtraction by calculating 546 – 289 is no different from doing 537 – 266. And even when they do, teachers and children have to be alert to variation that may be more than incidental. Tamara Bibby (2010) gives an example of a series of calculations in a textbook presented across the page in pairs with similar variation. The children are not sure whether to work across the pairs or down the page and seek the teacher's advice, who tells them to work down the page. Thus the textbook authors' presumed attempt to direct awareness is missed, along with the opportunity for mindful activity. If our goal is to drill children in reaching the point of 'mindless-ness' – of needing to attend to how to do the calculation with as much consciousness as, say, attending to writing your name – then indeed there is no point in making a distinction.

But there are the direct and indirect objects of learning in play here. I am arguing for using such calculations not just to get to the answer but also to raise learners' awareness of mathematical structure. The indirect object is for children to become mindful learners of mathematics. Examples like this are not merely about working on subtraction but also on the awareness that mathematical activity is full of possibility, full of potential that makes it interesting and engaging. The object of being able to correctly complete pages of calculations is left over from the Victorians when it was likely that some children were going to be going on to be clerks and spend their working lives having to fill ledgers with accurate calculations. But that is not the reality of life now – technology is now much more suited to calculating answers than humans, a fact of life that is even more likely to be the case in coming years.

Children are also being encouraged to be mindful through the different, conditional, readings of the subtraction sign: 546 – 289 could be subtraction as take-away, or it could be finding the difference between the two numbers. I want learners to bring this sense of conditionality to other calculations. 3004 – 1996 could be a 'take-away' or it could be 'find the difference' – choosing which of these readings to work with cannot only affect the likelihood of getting the answer correct but also raise calculations up from mere drill and practice. 'Ticket sales' further illustrates this.

Ticket sales

This problem was set up as a collaborative clue problem: working in pairs the children were given a clue each on separate slips of paper. Both clue cards had the problem set out on them but each had a different clue. The instructions to the children were that they could tell each other what was on their clue card but not show each other.

Ticket sales

Robbie Williams is performing in London.
Tickets sell quickly.
How many tickets are still on sale?

continued . . .

Clue 1:
5003 tickets are on sale.

Clue 2:
4997 tickets have been sold.

On the surface this looks like a very routine and not very exciting 'word problem' but it is subtler than that. The variation between the 'action' of the problem and the mathematically most effective way of solving it is key. The action of the story is one of taking away – a certain number of tickets are available to start, a number are removed through sales, how many remain? The immediate horizontal mathematizing leads to calculating a 'take-away' 5003 – 4997. Setting this out as a formal calculation and using a standard algorithm leads to a not very attractive calculation to carry out.

However, in carrying out the calculation, in working with the mathematics rather than with the 'real' world, it is more efficient to make a vertical shift in mathematizing. Given the numbers involved it is mathematically more effective to treat the calculation as finding a difference 4997 + [ ] = 5003

We were interested in whether or not the children would carry out the calculation in line with the real-world situation or whether they would have the awareness that there was a more effective way of calculating. Would the variation that we built in between the 'real' world (of imaginary ticket sales as taking away) and the 'mathematical' world (of subtraction as finding the difference) help the children become mindful of movements between the two?

Not surprisingly, many children immediately set out a formal algorithm. As the work samples show (Figure 10.8) this is not always successful. These two children quickly arrived at their answer, falling into the trap of saying 'you can't take a larger

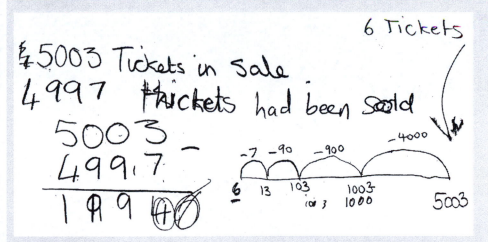

Figure 10.8 How many tickets are still on sale? (1)

continued . . .

number from a smaller number' and so in carrying out the calculation column by column arriving at a rather large answer. We had been working on using empty number lines so I asked this pair to check their answer in that way. The error of their ways became clear to them!

Some children chose to use an empty number line immediately and did find a correct solution. The method in Figure 10.9 shows strategic thinking. Rather than subtract 4,000 as we might expect, the children jumped back 4,003 to land on 1,000. Subtracting 900 was then easy, and 94 from 100 could be done in one step. (Although it would have been nice if they'd gone from right to left rather than left to right!)

Only one pair of quiet children treated the calculation as a 'find the difference' figuring out the answer with two jumps of three (Figure 10.3).

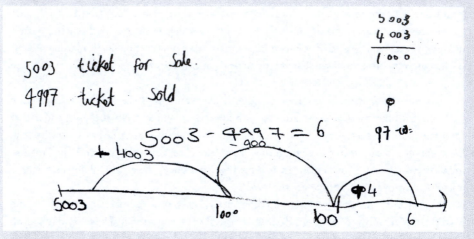

Figure 10.9 How many tickets are still on sale? (2)

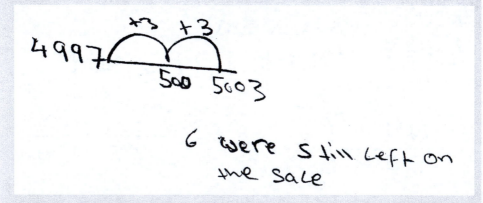

Figure 10.10 How many tickets are still on sale? (3)

continued . . .

When this pair followed two others in presenting their method, one of the other children quickly and loudly announced 'Hang on, that's not taking away that's finding the difference!' We asked the children to discuss in their pairs whether they thought it was okay to figure this out in a way that was different from that suggested by the story, and which of the methods they had seen presented they thought was most sensible. Coming back together as a class to talk about what they'd discussed there was general consensus that what the two quiet children had done was not only okay but also rather smart.

From models of to models for

It is important to monitor and assess children's use of models and look for evidence for when they make the move from using them as *models of* to being *models for* and then to becoming *tools for* thinking with. There are subtleties in the ways the children will be using these and being alert to the subtleties can help us judge when the children are making progress. Sally's and Tim's work on multiplication shows how in the space of one lesson children can progress from using an image as a model for to being a model of and being very close to it, then being a tool for thinking with.

Sally and Tim

Sally and her class of fellow nine-year-olds had been working with arrays to explore multiplication. They had been using these as models of multiplying together two single digits. As they had committed a number of the multiplication facts to memory, we moved to using the array as a model of multiplying a single digit by a teen number. The teacher had set up the model of splitting the teen number into a ten and a single digit and using this partitioning to find the total product. Figure 10.11 shows Sally's workings.

In question 4, Sally used the squared paper to represent 9×26 quite literally: her array is 9 squares by 26. We cannot tell from her representation if she used this as a *model of* or a *model for*: she may have counted all the individual squares to find the product (model of), or used her knowledge of multiplying by ten to calculate the partial products of 9×20 and 9×6 (model for).

Question 5 is much less ambiguous. Being so much smaller, this is clearly not a model of the multiplication as there is no way that Sally could have been counting squares. It is a model for.

To check out whether this marked a shift in her thinking, I asked Sally if she thought it was possible to use an array to multiply together 14 and 15. This time I gave her some plain paper to work on, so that counting squares would not be possible. Figure 10.12 shows her working.

Sally produced this quite unaided, apart from one small interaction. She drew the rectangle and sketched in the vertical line to partition the 15 into 10 and 5. She went to draw the horizontal line but paused and looked at me, as though for reassurance that this was acceptable. A slight nod from me and she drew the line, wrote in the four partial products and found the total. Her representation convinces me that she was reasoning

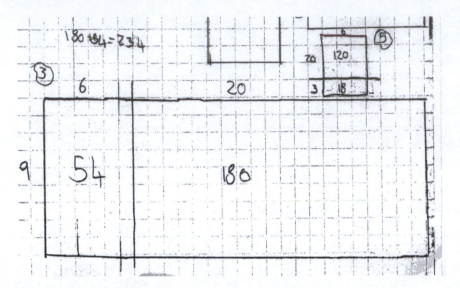

Figure 10.11 Sally's workings

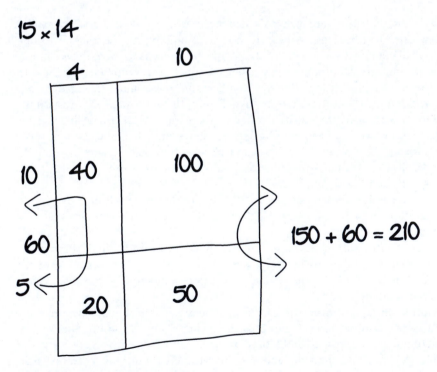

Figure 10.12 Sally's invented method

through here and not simply replicating some image that she had previously seen: the 'iconic' way of presenting this would look like Figure 10.13, with both tens in the upper left-hand corner, which is not how Sally presented it.

Tim's work shows another example of the move from a *model of* to a *model for*. One of his calculations was 9 × 16 and he told me he could remember that the answer to this was 99. I said we could check that and that I'd show him what I thought was a quick way of doing this. I modeled carrying out the calculation by setting up the array for 10 × 16 and then 'slicing off' a strip of 16 to find 9 × 16 (Figure 10.14).

15 × 14

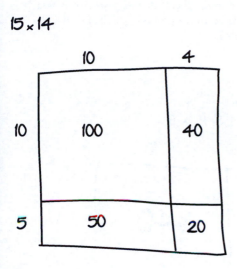

Figure 10.13 Standard grid method

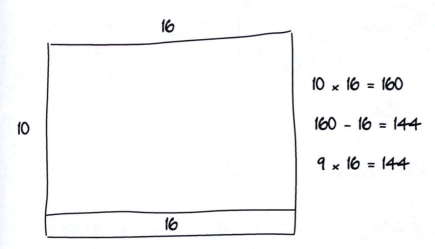

Figure 10.14 16 × 9

Although somewhat disappointed that the answer was not 99, Tim was pleased with this method and I asked him if he thought he could use it to calculate 9 × 22 and 34 × 9. Figure 10.15 shows his working.

It is possible that Tim had momentarily been able to recreate versions of the image he had just seen me produce, and so was working with a model of. The details of his representations suggest that he was treating this as a model for thinking through a solution, not simply mimicking. We had been consistent when working with arrays in always having the first number in the multiplication representing the number of rows and the second the number of columns. Tim is consistent with this: the first calculation represents 10 rows and 22 columns, the second 34 rows and 10 columns for the other. That required him to coordinate where to make each 'slice': in the first case it is across the array, mirroring my representation, but in the second case he has to take off a vertical 'slice', something that is not immediately obvious.

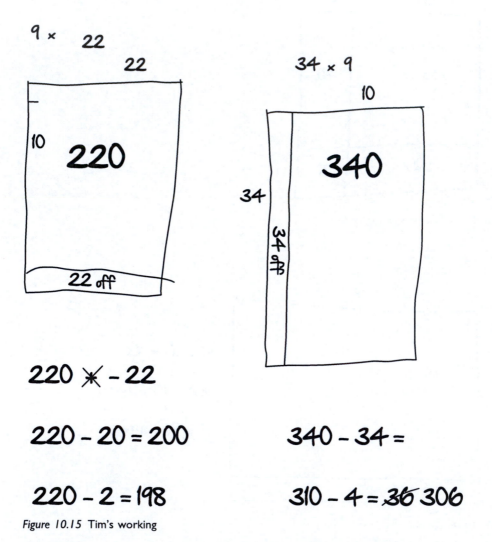

Figure 10.15 Tim's working

Here again the variation in the choice of examples challenges and reveals more than 22 × 9 and 34 × 9 would have done, both of which would only have required Tim to produce images very similar to mine.

Arrays in mind

For children to reach the point of *models for* that Sally and Tim demonstrate means children creating arrays as *models of* a variety of contexts: for example finding total numbers of pies on a tray, given the number of rows and the number of pies in each row. Or the number of stickers or stamps laid out in an array. Tasks included displaying images and children working in pairs with one partner sitting with their back to the image: the other child had to describe the array – could the child not able to see the image sketch something similar? From such tasks we moved to ones where the total number of items in an array could not all be seen, such as 'Stamps'.

Stamps

The narrative that we set up for this was my having an interest in stamp collecting and buying sheets of stamps in arrays. Sadly, I was not very careful in tidying these away and I would often come home to find that my dog, Max, had chewed up some of the stamps. Could the children figure out how many had been in a sheet before Max got to them?

From the experience of describing arrays, the children were able to mentally re-construct partial images like those in Figure 10.16:

 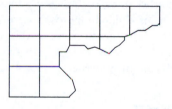

Figure 10.16 Torn grids (1)

Varying this to push their awareness, we also presented images like these:

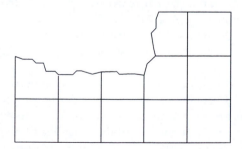

Figure 10.17 Torn grids (2)

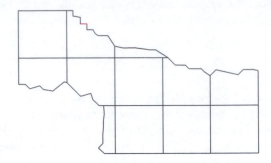

Figure 10.18 Torn grids (3)

The children initially found these difficult – how could they figure out how many stamps had originally been there when they could not 'see' how many rows there were, or how many there were in the top row? Working on imagining what they could see if the images were rotated shifted their awareness from the expectation that only the top or left-hand side were relevant. Images like those in Figure 10.18 where there were no complete rows or column pushed their reasoning still further.

Once the children were confident in describing and recreating arrays we explored playing around with partitioning arrays, recording the different multiplications and attending to the result that the overall totals remained unchanged. For example we set the task of drawing on squared paper a 5 × 7 array. What happens when you slice this array into two smaller ones, such as 5 × 5 and 5 × 2? Was the total the same? Working with this image helps children approach learning their multiplication bonds mindfully: I may not know 9 × 6 but I can think of this as 5 × 6 plus 4 × 6.

This extended exposure to working with and thinking about arrays also lays foundations for division, as 'Grandma's sweets' demonstrates.

Grandma's sweets

This example comes from a lesson introducing division to a class of eight-year-olds with experience of describing and working with arrays. The context for the lesson was inspired by Pat Hutchinson's story 'when the doorbell rang'. The plot of her story is about a mother baking and more and more people arriving every time she wants to share out her cakes. In our version we started by talking about grandparents coming to visit and how they often bring sweets. I told the children about a day that I could remember when my grandmother arrived with a bag of 24 sweets. There was my sister Mary, our brother Tom and myself at home so we decided to share the sweets out. Could the children figure out how many we each got?

Just as most of the children were getting to the point of finding 8 as the answer, I stopped them and continued to tell them that I could remember that day clearly because just as we were about to eat the sweets our other sister Jane arrived. Of course we could not miss her out, so we put the sweets back in the bag and shared them out again. And just as the class were finding the answer this: 'Guess what?' 'Oh no,' came the groans, 'someone else arrived'. 'That's right, our cousins, the twins. So we had to start again.'

The children set about repeatedly doing the sharing with great goodwill; largely I like to think because of the narrative structure within which we embedded the string of calculations.

What we had not anticipated was the number of children who, without any prompting, created images that set out the calculations in an array form (Figure 10.19). Using arrays as models for multiplication had enabled them to appropriate these to use as models for division.

The array supports making connections in multiplication and division, just as the empty number lines support making connections in addition and subtraction. Had we emphasized repeated addition as the main model for multiplication then that does not link so easily with division as sharing problems. You can model the quotitioning aspect of division – division as repeated subtraction – on a number line. A problem like 'I have a pot of 24 sweets and I want to make up party bags with 8 sweets in each bag. How many bags can I make up?' lends itself to repeatedly subtracting eight. However, to

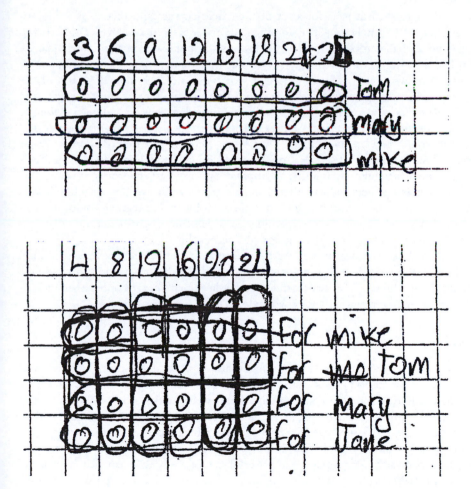

Figure 10.19 Using arrays to solve division problems

model 'share 24 sweets equally between 3 children' on a number line requires reasoning along the lines of repeatedly subtracting three (one for each of the three children) and then counting up the number of times that three was subtracted: not the lines that in my experience eight-year-olds reason along. But these children were able to reason using the array.

Collective use of representations

When I was at school there was little in the way of mathematics on display – after all if you opened up any child's exercise book they would all look pretty much the same (give or take the odd ink blot). Now, I do see some wonderful displays of mathematics in schools and these can be an inspiration for children and a great celebration of the mathematical activity that has gone on. But I also want to argue for the public display of work in progress. A class I visited in New York convinced me of the power of children keeping a record of their mathematics and displaying the work in progress as a resource for the whole class.

The children worked in pairs for a lot of their mathematics and there was a copious supply of cheap A3 'butcher's paper' for them to try ideas out on. Rather than being scrunched up and discarded at the end of lessons, or put away in trays, each pair of children had a section on a low display board that they pinned their sheets up on. Over the course of a few weeks, each new sheet of workings would be pinned on top of the existing ones creating something like a large flipbook of workings. Three things came out from this. First the children could look back at what they had done previously. Rather than assume (or hope) that a representation they had created that was successful and helpful would stick in their minds, they were there to go back to, borrow from, build on and refine. Just as artists swear by their sketchbooks and writers by their journals for inspiration, these children could be re-inspired by their earlier records.

Second, by making them public rather than private, they also were a valuable resource for the rest of the class. If a group got stuck on a problem, the teacher could say 'you know I think Liza and Sammy did something last week that might be an idea that you could use' and the children could easily go and access this.

Last but not least, the display was a great assessment tool for the teacher. She could look back over the records in chronological order and see the progression in children's approaches. (The children also had exercise books in which they recorded their tidied-up solutions to mathematics that they worked on.)

Summary

Introducing models such as the empty number line or array takes time. Children will only come to appreciate the power of these through repeated exposure to them and then it takes them different times to come to take them on as models for working with and then as tools for thinking. Such models are not 'topics' that are introduced and 'done' in the space of two or three weeks. They need to become part of the pedagogical 'furniture' of classrooms, as ubiquitous as paper and pencil. For me they are the mathematical equivalent of phonics – a powerful set of tools that can help you make sense of mathematical activity. But phonics only go so far; they can help you 'spell out' (some) English words, they do not represent the whole of being literate. And powerful though these mathematical models and tools are, they only reach their full potential in the presence of the third leg of the teaching tripod: talk.

Further reading

Young Mathematicians at Work: Constructing Number Sense, Addition and Subtraction, Young Mathematicians at Work: Constructing Multiplication and Division, Young Mathematicians at Work: Constructing Fractions, Decimals and Percentages by Cathy Fosnot and Marteen Dolk. These three books have a wealth of detail on models at a level that there is not room for here. Highly recommended.

Chapter 11

Talk

The first time this happened to me I was a student of composer Easley Blackwood in Chicago; part of my apprenticeship was listening to him practice piano, often for many hours at a sitting. As our attunement grew, I found I could follow his practice routines and his patient polishing of passages under study. One fine day (actually it was three in the morning) I realized that I was on his wavelength. Not only was I hearing as he was, I was hearing through his ears. . . .

I think this strange sensation is what happens when you listen long and quietly. It is a way of being helped, and of helping.

(Mathieu 1991)

This chapter examines the third leg of the teaching tripod: talk. I present the case for talk, and equally important, listening, attuning learners to mathematical themes and building a harmonious community.

Much talk in mathematics lessons stops short at children sharing their finished methods. The emphasis is on children reporting already complete mathematics and the talk resembles a series of monologues, with one child offering their solution followed by another. The other class members are cast as passive listeners, or, at best, good listeners, which usually means looking attentive and not interrupting. Children need to be active listeners, attending to and then attuning to the messages from their peers and becoming mindful of connections with their own emergent understandings and mathematical voice. Where speaking and listening are both well established in classroom activity, dialogue can occur in which mathematical ideas are invoked, arranged, expressed, and played with until the collective understanding is well pitched. When pupils are attuned to and thinking about each other's methods then it is possible that a dialogue unfolds about the relative benefits of different methods and, say, which are more effective, rather than simply whether or not they are correct. Mathematical meaning emerges through giving voice to tasks and tools: without talk mathematical images are silent, like notes on a sheet of music. Musicians know the difference between printed notes and live music. Mathematicians know the difference between written symbols and doing maths. Learning mathematics is coming to know this difference. Talk is how we come to that knowing. Talk that supports collective mathematical activity is distinguished by

- emphasizing listening as well as speaking
- recognizing the difference between discussion and dialogue
- focusing on mathematical reasoning as much as answers.

The importance of listening

In a class I visited, the teacher put a calculation on the board and asked the children to explain to a partner how they had found the answer. Sitting down next to two boys, I listened as the first one explained his method. When he finished I asked his partner what he thought.

B:	I agree
MA:	Agree with what?
B:	With what he said
MA:	What did he say?
B:	How he worked it out
MA:	How did he work it out?
B:	The way he said he did.

Had I pursued this conversation I am sure it would have gone round in circles. The boy had given all the signs of listening – turned toward, eye contact, head nods – but had not engaged with what his partner was saying. I suspect he was doing what I catch myself doing when waiting for a turn to speak: mentally rehearsing what I am going to say when I get the airspace.

This may be no bad thing: each pupil gets a chance to articulate his or her thinking – saying ideas out loud consolidates them. But pupil talk can go much further. Attending to each other's ideas is more important when using paired work to develop understanding or problem solving. If each speaker is simply talking 'to the air' then the conversation is not likely to spiral up and help participants develop their understanding.

Children listening, really listening, to a partner is not something we can take for granted. It needs to be worked on and constantly refined – it is not a 'one-off' emphasis at the beginning of the year but needs attending to and developing throughout the year (indeed throughout schooling).

Part of this involves helping children appreciate the value in listening to each other. Research by Jenny Young-Loveridge and her colleagues found that while some children thought it was important to explain their methods to each other, many of the same children thought that it wasn't important to listen to other children's methods (Young-Loveridge, Taylor *et al.* 2006). Are our classrooms full of children that think their methods are important, but that no one else's are as important?

Discussion or dialogue

At the heart of learning to listen is the distinction between being involved in a discussion or in a dialogue. Robin Alexander espouses the importance of 'dialogic teaching' in which the classroom participants (including the teacher) are engaged in productive talk about what is being learned (Alexander 2006). Is dialogue simply a synonym for classroom talk, or the frequently used discussion?

Dialogue comes from the Greek dialogos. 'Logos' – 'the word', and 'dia' – 'through'; hence meaning is created *through* the word – not *in* the words. Knowing comes about through the building and bartering, the back and forth exchanges of a dialogue, as opposed to knowledge being packaged up in words and passed across. And a dialogue can involve many more than two people as often supposed.

David Bohm, the physicist turned philosopher, contrasts the origins of dialogue with those of discussion (Bohm 2004). Discussion shares a common etymological root with percussion and concussion (that must be why so many discussions leave me with a headache). Discussion, Bohm suggests, is about breaking things up, with 'point scoring' often involved. In discussion the participants usually have a pre-determined position that they hold to. Discussion is about trying to establish this position (or shift another's). Discussion is largely a win–lose game play.

Dialogue has a different play to it. It's not about trying to win – it's an exchange of views, an attempt to understand the other better, rather than to try and impose one's view upon the other. Peter Senge talks of the importance in dialogue of holding a point of view 'gently' (Senge 2006). Lois Holzman talks of the importance of pointless conversations – not in the sense of them being meaningless or without purpose, but in the sense of not trying to get a particular point across (Holzman 2009). The paraphernalia of teaching objectives and learning outcomes can militate against the possibility of 'pointless' conversations in mathematics lessons. Dialogue also goes beyond coming to know. Richard Bernstein writes that 'dialogic communication presupposes moral virtues – a certain "good will" – at least in the willingness to really listen, to seek to understand what is genuinely other, different, alien, and the courage to risk one's more cherished prejudgments' (Bernstein 1992: 51).

The mathematics education literature acknowledges the importance of children speaking – explaining their methods – and listening. But speaking and listening is usually enlisted in support of the cognitive. Bernstein draws our attention to the fact that there is a moral dimension to speaking and listening. The child who acts to exclude a member of the group – what are they learning about helping others, valuing diversity and listening deeply? And what is the child learning about him- or her-self? What sort of 'character' is being allowed to develop and flourish in such circumstances? What of the child cast into and accepting the role of passive, excluded, silent observer? We must not tacitly sanction, in the name of higher standards, behaviors in mathematics lessons that are morally dubious and would not be accepted elsewhere.

Dialogue, rather than discussion, in mathematics lessons can be a challenge – after all there are still right answers in mathematics. Answers depend on questions and it's generally taken that preparation of 'good' questions is an essential part of effective mathematics teaching. This emphasis on questioning may not be the best way to foster dialogue. James Dillon has shown that children respond better to talking about statements than answering questions (Dillon 1985). Contrary to what we might expect, teacher questions close down options while statements can lead to more dialogue, deeper involvement, broader participation and richer arguments. Getting children to talk about whether they consider a statement such as

All squares are rectangles

is always, sometimes or never true, can produce a richer dialogue than posing the question

Is a square a rectangle?

There is more conditionality in a statement, more invitation to be mindful. Questions can have an air of testing what has been remembered rather than inviting meaning making.

Reasoning

In the examples throughout this book, I have stressed the importance of children developing the mathematical practices of reasoning, explaining and justifying. When teaching I frequently ask children to 'turn to your partner, share your answers and explain how you got them'. I do this so that children have plenty of opportunities to rehearse their explanations and to hear a partner's version. I cannot emphasize enough the importance of lessons being constantly peppered with turn-and-talk – I expect children to engage in such conversations whoever they are sitting next to, friend or foe. The only time I don't ask the children to turn-and-talk is when I expect them to be fluent in answering. For example, I expect most eight-year-olds to fluently add 10 or a small multiple of 10 to any two-digit number. 'Forty-seven add twenty' 'sixty-seven' is a rapid question-and-response routine. Turn-and-talk is not appropriate here because it gives the wrong message – that the children should be aware of how they found the answer – and, for those children who are fluent, explaining how they got the answer is not possible. They 'just know' and may end up creating explanations for the sake of it. An explanation has to be about gaining insight and, occasionally, just knowing is fine. Turn-and-talk, or not, helps signal these changes of expectation.

It's popularly believed that children need to be taught 'basic' skills before they can solve problems requiring them to explain and justify. I do not find this to be the case, although I do interpret explaining broadly – using practical materials, drawing pictures, creating diagrams, describing in words, and, of course, using symbols. Not that I count anything shown practically or on paper as evidence of children explaining or justifying. I'm looking for tasks that engage children in activity that is at the 'growing edge' of what they can do. 'Socks and Sticks' (see Chapter 5) does, I think, show six-year-olds explaining, since they did not simply 'know the answer'. The marks they made on paper helped them to find the solution; they did not record a solution that they had already found. The records, in the making of them, were an 'extension' of the mind. The records also provide the stimulus for whole-class dialogue. In contrast, an eight-year-old who quickly knew the answer to each problem might produce similar images if asked to 'convince me' but was hardly likely to be using the images to think through how they got those answers. Explaining and justifying has to be as much something that is in the moment, a form of external thinking (with props such as cubes or paper and pencil) through talk, which subsequently becomes a post hoc reconstruction.

Reasoning helps with generalizing – moving away from the specific examples, to speculating about underlying regularity. Generalizing moves children's awareness from the direct object of an activity to an indirect object. A core activity here is conjecturing. A conjecture is a yet-to-be-proved statement rather than a definitive statement of the answer.

Mathematicians work with conjectures all the time. In lessons marked by a conjecturing approach, you see the class debating and deciding whether offerings are correct or not, rather than the teacher filtering and judging answers. Teacher-as-judge-of-correctness is an easy role to adopt. It is harder to adopt a 'neutral' stance and make the collective responsible for deciding what is correct. It means accepting all answers as conditional, listing them without comment, noting that they cannot all be right and asking children to discuss, first in pairs and then as a class, which they think are correct.

In fact, children do often engage in conjecturing, although they do not call it that. When children feel safe offering answers that they might be unsure of, they will often answer a question with another question: 'Is it . . .?' One option for the teacher is to answer the question – 'yes it is', or perhaps, 'think a bit more about that' (code for 'no, it isn't'). Listening out for such conditional responses from the children provides a way into developing conjecturing as a core activity. 'Ok, Libby thinks it might be 45. Let's jot that down. Does anyone think that as well? What other answers do we have?' Note that I'm not assuming Libby's answer is wrong; conjecturing is not a 'holding' activity until the correct answer is elicited.

Private talk and public conversation

To promote this dialogic, conversational approach to mathematics talk, I have argued that there need to be two aspects to talk in mathematics classrooms:

- private talk in pairs or small groups
- public conversation as a class.

The former provides the opportunity for children to 'buy in' to the mathematics being discussed, share their thinking in a secure setting and rehearse ideas that they might share more widely. In the latter the whole class shares and builds on ideas. As this is necessarily more risky than private talk, the private talk is a necessary precursor to the public conversation being effective. Let's look at each of these in detail.

Private talk

I mentioned earlier that if children are used to mathematics as an individual activity then they might be reluctant initially to share ideas. Some structured tasks that can help children listen more actively in paired work include:

- paired calculations
- solver-recorder
- clue problem.

PAIRED CALCULATIONS

When children are working on the same calculation, and have each arrived at the answer, then they may be eager to share their method but, since they each have an answer and a method, the benefits of listening to someone else's strategy are not immediately clear. Putting two different but similar calculations on the board and asking pairs to each do one of the calculations and then take turns to explain their solution to their partner can promote more authentic listening. Since their partner does not have a vested interest in the same calculation there is a more genuine need to explain and listen.

SOLVER-RECORDER

Provide one piece of paper and pen between two. Children take it in turns to be the solver – they have to do the figuring out – while their partner has to do the recording. The solver has to explain what to write down and their partner has to record what they are asked to record – they cannot take over the solving of the problem even if their partner gets stuck. (Children I've worked with like to call this solver-robot. The robot can only record.) What I've found actually happens is that the child acting as recorder, once their partner has finished, spontaneously starts to record what they would have done, but having acted as recorder they are more likely to relate their solution method to what their partner did, either building on this or providing an alternative. For example, Figure 11.1 shows what a seven-year-old recorded when her partner was figuring out the difference between 50 and 160. Her partner had asked her to draw the number line with 50 at one end and 160 at the other. He then asked her to draw the jump of 40 from 50 to 90 and could then figure out that the second jump would be 70, giving a difference of 110. Released from her role as recorder, the girl drew her solution: add on 50 to 100 and then 60, again giving 110 as the difference.

CLUE PROBLEM

The example of 'ticket sales' (Chapter 10) was set up as a clue problem. Creating your own examples is easy. Find a typical 'word problem' (National Tests are a good source) and split the information in the problem into two parts. Put this partial information on two separate pieces of paper together with the question. Take this example:

> Russell buys a sandwich for £3.50 and two cokes for £1.25 each. How much change does he get from a £10 note?

Each clue could have the question:

> How much change does Russell get from a £10 note?

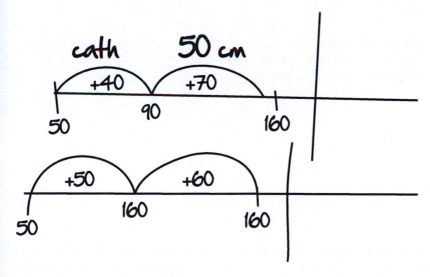

Figure 11.1 Solver and recorder

Clue 1 could be:

Russell buys a sandwich for £3.50

Clue 2 could be:

Russell buys two cokes for £1.25 each

Working in pairs, children get one 'clue' each and jointly solve the problem. They can read out what is on their 'clue' card but must not show it to their partner. The reading out encourages listening and the 'not showing' rule stops one child simply handing everything over to their partner to do the work.

Public conversation

Private paired talk is only part of the story. Bringing the paired work together in a whole class conversation provides the opportunity to build on children's methods, refine the mathematics and reach collective understanding.

Many whole-class public conversations I've heard go along the lines of 'how many different methods can we find?' to the point where children start inventing methods for the sake of it. In one class children were explaining how they calculated the price of two chocolate bars costing 24p each. The first methods offered were ones that you might expect such as adding 20 + 20 and 4 + 4 and then adding 40 and 8 or doubling 25 and taking off 2. A child then claimed that they had halved 96. My suspicion was that the child had worked back from knowing that the answer was 96 and was not actually describing what they had done. The teacher praised her for suggesting another interesting method.

Rather than examine a range of solutions, we need to work with children to understand and closely examine one or two solution. This provides the 'bedrock' for the conversations with other solutions subsequently building or being contrasted to these particular solutions.

Building on the work of Robin Alexander (2006) and Neil Mercer (1995, 2000) I find the following rubric helpful in managing the whole class, public, conversation and focusing the children on particular methods:

- Rehearse
- Revoice
- Repeat
- Rephrase
- Build on
- Comment on.

REHEARSE

When it comes to whole-class conversations, I don't ask for volunteers. Partly because I don't want the same children to always explain, but more importantly, I want explanations that sound likely to start a good conversation. While the children are still working in pairs, I go round listening in to their conversations and listening out for rich – not necessarily correct but full of potential for generating conversation – solutions. I am listening to select two, perhaps three solutions that may be contrasting or cumulative.

A Japanese primary teacher used a similar technique in a lesson I watched. Planning for the lesson, he had carefully chosen a problem and thought through the three or four solution methods the children were most likely to come up with. Using this he had prepared a table listing the children's names with these different solution methods heading up columns. As the teacher moved around the room he could mark off on his chart the method that each child used. In the plenary the teacher used this information to choose which children to invite to explain; he also had a snapshot record of the children's thinking.

Telling children in advance that they are going to be sharing their thinking with the rest of the class means that they have time to rehearse what they are going to say and the class then hears a more coherent explanation.

REVOICE

Standing in front of the class, even with the opportunity to rehearse, children reveal the difficulties in explaining for others. The talk that gave rise to personal meaning is not easily transformed into a public performance that others can follow.

The teacher plays a key part in supporting this private–public transition. I recommend two strategies. First, move to the back of the class, so this does not turn into a private conversation at the board. Standing up at the front of the class is daunting for many children – positioning yourself at the back of the class says 'OK, you are now the teacher'. You can also direct their performance from there with comments like 'I can't hear you back here, you need to speak up.'

Second, listen to the quality of the explanation and interject at points where you think clarity is needed. This is difficult because we all 'fill in the gaps' in conversations. Having listened to the private talk and chosen these particular children to explain, you'll already have understood their method and it is easy to listen through that framework of understanding. You have to listen as though hearing their explanation for the first time, and to intervene in ways that will help the children to clarify their explanation, but without taking the explanation away from them. It is easy, through the desire to move things along, to say things like 'what I think you are trying to say is . . .' and take over, giving your explanation. Better to say things like:

> 'Hang on, you said you did . . . and then (something else). I don't follow this – how did you get from that first thing to the next?'

or

> 'I'm a bit confused. Is anyone else? Can you explain that bit again please?'

REPEAT

Once children have shared their thinking with the class, it's helpful to get others to simply repeat what has been said. I say 'simply', but children find this surprisingly hard. If the explanation is brief it is worth insisting on an accurate repetition of what was said, not an approximation. Put it back to the children up front to decide if there was an accurate repetition. 'Is that what you said? No? OK, then tell us again, and Sandy, listen really carefully so you can say it exactly the same.' It may appear pedantic but sticking with a child, not letting them off this listening hook, until everyone agrees that an accurate repetition is arrived at does pay off.

There are three reasons for this pedantry. First to emphasize that careful listening is being valued and that this is not easy but that, with patience, it can be done. Second, there is power in voicing another's words. Repeating something even if it is not fully fathomed throws out a line that catches at understanding. Third, everyone gets to listen to the same explanation a few times over. Even with the best listening in the world it is unlikely that all will have 'got it' first time round.

REPHRASE

Once everyone is agreed on what has been offered, invite children to explain what they heard in their own words. This encourages others to take some ownership of the maths and begins to open up the conversation. As before, the children giving the original explanation decide if their peers rephrase accurately.

At each stage – revoicing, repeating, rephrasing – invite questions; aim for collective understanding of what is offered. Note that the offering is still accepted as it is – not yet judging whether the solution is right or wrong, effective or efficient, common or unique, although often errors do surface and have been tidied up by this point.

BUILD ON

Repeating and rephrasing leads into building on the solution comes about through questions like:

• Does anyone want to add anything to that method?
• Did anyone do anything similar to that?

Building on helps to fill gaps in a solution or unearth further errors. The focus is now firmly on this publicly shared solution and not on the individuals proposing it.

COMMENT ON

This phase opens out the dialogue and invites more discussion about the mathematics of the solution. Again, the time spent talking about the one method and reaching some general communal understanding of it is to encourage shared ownership – the idea is now the class's idea to work on and talk about, not simply that of two particular children. This is a key step in creating a mathematics-focused community rather than a teacher-focused or child-focused one.

Summary

Talk is central to mathematics lessons. Children are not talking *about* mathematics, but are *talking mathematics*, just as there is a difference between talking about Italian and talking Italian. Talking mathematics means that mathematical vocabulary becomes part of the classroom discourse. It's not a list of words that you select from to put your ideas 'into': it is the words through which ideas are formed. The skilful teacher promotes talking mathematics by offering mathematically worthwhile tasks, accepting what children say in the course of activity on these tasks, and supporting them to craft their talk into mathematical objects to share. This sounds difficult but is something parents instinctively do when talking with young children. They accept the talk that the child produces but the adult's response is a little more sophisticated. Parents don't always overtly correct the child. To a child saying 'want bikkie' an attuned parent responds 'you would like a biscuit?' The adult models in response to the child's attempt, building on what the child brings. Parents don't go round saying, 'right, today I'm going to teach you how to ask for a biscuit. You say, "Can I have a biscuit please?" Now try asking for some milk'. The children's offering is the starting point and the growing point.

This may sound like a laissez-faire discovery approach; just wait (and hope) for the child to say something about taking away and then pick up on that and talk about subtraction. It is not laissez-faire. It is planned, it is structured. The planning comes through the careful choice of tasks and the structuring through subsequent tool use in mathematical activity. Out of the informal, improvised solutions that children produce comes the ore of mathematics that can be panned, collectively polished and crafted into nuggets of mathematics.

Making sense of problems by explaining them to somebody else, putting them in your own words and comparing your answer with others all help meaning to emerge. As one pupil was recently quoted as saying, 'Working with someone else helps you understand, especially if they ask you questions' (Ofsted 2008).

Further reading

Towards Dialogic Teaching: Rethinking Classroom Talk by Robin Alexander. A brief and readable introduction to the theory and evidence for the centrality of talk in learning. Not just about mathematics but the centrality of dialogue across the curriculum.

Using Discussion in Classrooms by James Dillon. This seems to be out of print but, if you can get hold of it, it is a valuable guide to managing large-group discussions.

Coda

There's a fourth T that sits alongside the tripod of Tasks, Tools and Talk. That T is Trust.

Changing teaching is risky, and risk taking means trusting that the outcomes will be worth the risk. If we want children to engage with mindful, meaningful mathematical tasks then we, teachers, have to trust that they will come up with improvised solutions that can be collectively crafted into the canonical mathematics. They, the children, have to trust that we are genuinely interested in their thinking. And we have to trust ourselves to be able to make sense of what the children produce.

A key to developing such mutual trust lies in a shift of the 'division of labor' in mathematics lessons. Mathematics lessons are often structured around

- the teacher explaining
- the children following the explanation.

In mindful mathematics lessons the shift is to

- someone explaining
- everyone following the explanation.

It's not that the teacher never explains, but that everyone in the community gets to be teacher and learner, whether they are adult or child.

Trust me, it works.

Acknowledgements

It has been my pleasure and privilege to work with so many talented and thoughtful teachers and researchers over the years, and I am bound to forget to thank everyone, so my apologies in advance to anyone inadvertently not included here.

Thanks to my colleagues at King's College, London. The mathematics education research group there, past and present, has helped form and develop my thinking in ways that I could never have anticipated, with help from David Johnson, Jeremy Hodgen, Alison Millett, Tamara Bibby, Diana Coben and Hazel Denvir. I cannot express enough gratitude to Margaret Brown for not only being the most generous scholar that I know, but also the wisest and most supportive.

Cathy Fosnot offered me the opportunity to work on her wonderful Mathematics in the City project: thanks for the trust she placed in me and the inspiration she and her colleagues provided.

Thanks to John Mason for sparking my initial interest in mathematics education and being a constant source of stimulation over the years.

Then there are the teachers who have so kindly granted me access to their classrooms: thanks to all of you who I cannot name personally. Amanda Phillips and the staff at Old Ford Primary School deserve especial thanks for the wonderful times teaching there, as does Penny Latham for helping develop many of the ideas here. Thanks to Lynne Churchman and the teachers in King Solomon Academy and Ark Academy. And thanks to all the other teachers in New York and in and around London that I've had the pleasure of working with.

To all the children who have put up with my trying to 'catch them out' – thanks and I hope at least a few of them have ended up pursuing mathematics.

Thanks to Graham Barker for the coffees and chats at Departures and the constant encouragement.

Thanks to Sheila Ebbutt for trying to break my habit of split infinitives and being such a wonderful colleague at BEAM.

Thanks to Lynne Maclure for being a wonderful colleague at conferences and for her inspirational mathematical activities.

Thanks to Joe Carter, editor of *Teach Primary* for permission to adapt some activities originally published there.

Last, but of course not least, thanks to Russell Knoll for not being there when I needed to withdraw and write, and for being there at all the other times.

References

Alexander, R. (2006) *Towards Dialogic Teaching: Rethinking Classroom Talk*. Cambridge: Dialogos.

Alexander, R. (ed.) (2010) *Children, Their World, Their Education: The Final Report and Recommendations of the Cambridge Primary Review*. London and New York: Routledge.

Anghileri, J. (ed.) (2001) *Principles and Practices in Arithmetic Teaching*. Buckingham, UK: Open University Press.

Askew, M. (2010) 'It ain't (just) what you do: effective teachers of numeracy', in I. Thompson, *Issues in Teaching Numeracy in Primary Schools (second edition)*. Buckingham, UK: Open University Press, pp. 91–102.

Askew, M., T. Bibby *et al.* (1997) *Raising Attainment in Numeracy: Final Report to Nuffield Foundation*. London: King's College, University of London.

Askew, M., T. Bibby and M. Brown (2002) *Mental Calculation: Interpretation and Implementation*. London: King's College, London, University of London.

Askew, M., M. Brown, V. Rhodes, D. Wiliam and D. Johnson (1997) *Effective Teachers of Numeracy: Report of a study carried out for the Teacher Training Agency*. London: King's College, University of London.

Ausubel, D. P. (1968) *Educational Psychology: A Cognitive View*. New York: Holt, Rinehart & Winston.

Ball, D. L. (1990) 'Prospective elementary and secondary teachers' understanding of division', *Journal for Research in Mathematics Education* 21(2): 132–144.

Ball, D. L. and H. Bass (2000) 'Interweaving content and pedagogy in teaching and learning to teach: knowing and using mathematics' in J. Boaler, *Multiple Perspectives on Mathematics Teaching and Learning*. Westport, CT: Ablex Publishing, pp. 83–104.

Ball, D. L. and H. Bass (2003) 'Toward a practice-based theory of mathematical knowledge for teaching', Proceedings of the 2002 annual meeting of the Canadian Mathematics Education Study Group, Edmonton, AB, CMESG/GDEDM.

Becker, H. S. (2000) 'The etiquette of improvisation', *Mind, Culture, and Activity* 7(3): 171–176.

Bellah, R. N., R. Madsen, W. M. Sullivan, A. Swidler and S. M. Tipton (1985) *Habits of the Heart: Individualism and Commitment in American Life*. New York: Harper & Row.

Benezet, L. P. (1935a) 'The Teaching of Arithmetic I: The Story of an Experiment', *Journal of the National Education Association* 24: 241–244.

Benezet, L. P. (1935b) 'The Teaching of Arithmetic II: The Story of an Experiment', *Journal of the National Education Association* 24: 301–303.

Benezet, L. P. (1935c) 'The Teaching of Arithmetic III: The Story of an Experiment', *Journal of the National Education Association* 25: 7–8.

Bernstein, R. (1992) *The New Constellation*. Cambridge, MA: MIT Press.

Bibby, T. (2010) *Education – An Impossible Profession? Psychoanalytic Explorations of Learning and Classrooms*. London: Routledge.

Bion, W. (1984) *Transformations (Maresfield Library)*. *New edition*. London: Karnac Books.

Bliss, J., M. Askew and S. Macrae (1996) 'Effective teaching and learning: Scaffolding revisited', *Oxford Review of Education* 22(1): 37–61.

Boaler, J. (1997) *Experiencing School Mathematics: Teaching styles, sex and setting*. Buckingham, UK: Open University Press.

Boaler, J. (1999) 'Participation, Knowledge and Beliefs: A Community Perspective on Mathematics Learning', *Educational Studies in Mathematics* 40(3): 259–281.

Bohm, D. (2004) *On Dialogue*. New York and Abingdon: Routledge Classics.

Bowden, J. and F. Marton (1998) *The University of Learning*. London: Kogan Page.

Brown, M., M. Askew, J. Hodgen, V. Rhodes and D. Wiliam (2003) 'Individual and cohort progression in learning numeracy ages 5–11: results from the Leverhulme 5-year longitudinal study', *Proceedings of the International Conference on Mathematics and Science Learning*. Taipei, Taiwan: 81–109.

Brown, S. I. and M. I. Walter (1990) *The Art of Problem Posing*. Hillsdale, NJ: Lawrence Erlbaum Associates.

Bruner, J. (1979) *On Knowing: Essays for the Left Hand*. Cambridge, MA: Harvard University Press.

Bruner, J. (1986) *Actual Minds, Possible Worlds*. London: Harvard University Press.

Bruner, J. (1996) *The Culture of Education*. Cambridge, MA and London: Harvard University Press.

Brynner, J. and S. Parsons (1997) *Does Numeracy Matter? Evidence from the National Child Development Study on the Impact of Poor Numeracy on Adult Life*. London: Basic Skills Agency.

Cadinu, M., A. Maass, A. Rosabianca and J. Kiesner (2005) 'Why Do Women Underperform Under Stereotype Threat? Evidence for the Role of Negative Thinking', *Psychological Science* 16(7): 275–278.

Cameron, A., M. Dolk, C. Twomey-Fosnot and S. B. Hersch (2005) *Exploring Soda Machines, Grades 3–5 (Resource Package, including CD-ROM)*. Portsmouth, NH: Heinemann.

Campbell, D. T. (1974) '"Downward causation" in hierarchically organized biological systems' in F. J. Ayala and T. Dobzhansky, *Studies in the Philosophy of Biology: Reduction and Related Problems*. Berkeley, CA: University of California Press, pp. 179–186.

Carr, N. (2010) *The Shallows*. London: Atlantic Books.

Cole, M. (1996) *Cultural Psychology: A Once and Future Discipline*. Cambridge, MA and London: The Belknap Press of Harvard University Press.

Cross, K. (2004) 'Engagement and excitement in mathematics', *Mathematics Teaching* 189: 4–6.

Csikszentmihalyi, M. (1990) *Flow: The Psychology of Optimal Experience*. New York: Harper Perennial.

Cuoco, A., E. P. Goldenberg and J. Mark (1996) 'Habits of mind: An organizing principle for a mathematics curriculum', *Journal of Mathematical Behavior* 15 (4): 375–402.

Davis, B. (1996) *Teaching Mathematics: Toward a Sound Alternative*. New York and London: Routledge.

Davis, B. and E. Simmt (2003) 'Understanding learning systems: mathematics education and complexity science', *Journal for Research in Mathematics Education* 34(2): 137–167.

Davis, B. and D. Sumara (2006) *Complexity and Education: Inquiries into Learning, Teaching and Research*. Mahwah, NJ and London: Lawrence Erlbaum Associates.

Davis, B., D. Sumara and R. Luce-Kapler (2000) *Engaging Minds: Learning and Teaching in a Complex World*. Mahwah, NJ: Lawrence Erlbaum Associates.

Dehaene, S. (1999) *The Number Sense: How the Mind Creates Mathematics*. Oxford: Oxford University Press.

Denvir, B. and M. Brown (1986a) 'Understanding of number concepts in low attaining 7–9 year olds: Part I. Development of descriptive framework and diagnostic instrument', *Educational Studies in Mathematics* 17: 15–36.

Denvir, B. and M. Brown (1986b) 'Understanding of number concepts in low attaining 7–9 year olds: Part II. The teaching studies', *Educational Studies in Mathematics* 17: 143–164.

Denvir, H. and T. Bibby (1997) *Diagnostic Interviews in Number Sense*. London: BEAM Education.

Department for Education and Employment (DfEE) (1999) *The National Numeracy Strategy: Framework for teaching mathematics from Reception to Year 6*. London: DfEE.

Dewey, J. (1956) *The Child and the Curriculum and The School and Society*. Chicago: University of Chicago Press.

Dillon, J. T. (1985) 'Using questions to foil discussion', *Teaching and Teacher Education* 1(2): 109–121.

Doidge, N. (2007) *The Brain That Changes Itself: Stories of Personal Triumph From the Frontiers of Brain Science*. London: Penguin.

Dweck, C. S. (2000) *Self-Theories: Their Role in Motivation, Personality, and Development*. Philadelphia: Psychology Press (Taylor and Francis Group).

Elbert, T., C. Pantev, C. Wienbruch, B. Rockstroh and E. Taub (1995) 'Increased cortical representation of the fingers of the left hand in string players', *Science* 270(5234): 305–307.

Fosnot, C. T. and M. Dolk (2001a) *Young Mathematicians at Work: Constructing Multiplication and Division*. Portsmouth, NH: Heinemann.

Fosnot, C. T. and M. Dolk (2001b) *Young Mathematicians at Work: Constructing Number Sense, Addition and Subtraction*. Portsmouth, NH: Heinemann.

Freudenthal, H. (1975) *Mathematics as an Educational Task*. Dordrecht, The Netherlands: Reidel.

Fullan, M. (2003) *The Moral Imperative of School Leadership*. Thousand Oaks, CA: Corwin Press.

Fullan, M. and A. Hargreaves (1996) *What's Worth Fighting For in Your School? (second edition)*. New York: Teachers College Press.

Fuson, K. C. and Y. Kwon (1992) 'Korean children's single-digit addition and subtraction: Numbers structured by ten', *Journal for Research in Mathematics Education* 23(2): 148–165.

Geary, D. C., C. C. Bow-Thomas, F. Liu and R. S. Siegler (1996) 'Development of Arithmetical Competencies in Chinese and American Children: Influence of Age, Language, and Schooling', *Child Development* 67(5): 2022–2044.

Gergen, K. (2009) *An Introduction to Social Construction (second edition)*. London: Sage Publications.

Giddens, A. (1991) *Modernity and Self-Identity. Self and Society in the Late Modern Age*. Cambridge: Polity.

Good, T. L. and J. E. Brophy (1997) *Looking in Classrooms*. New York: Longman.

Goswami, U. (2001) 'Cognitive development – no stages please – we're British', *British Journal of Psychology* 92.

Goswami, U. (2007) *Cognitive Development: The Learning Brain*. London: Psychology Press.

Goswami, U. and P. Bryant (2010) (Chapter 6) 'Children's cognitive development and learning' in R. J. Alexander, with C. Doddington, J. Gray, L. Hargreaves and R. Kershner, *The Cambridge Primary Review Research Surveys*. London: Routledge.

Gravemeijer, K. (1999) 'How emergent models may foster the constitution of formal mathematics', *Mathematical Thinking and Learning* 1(2): 155–177.

Griffin, P. (1989) 'Teaching Takes Place in Time, Learning Takes Place Over Time', *Mathematics Teaching* 126: 12–13.

Hart, K. (ed.) (1981) *Children's Understanding of Mathematics: 11–16*. London: John Murray.

Hart, K., D. C. Johnson, M. Brown, L. Dickson and R. Clarkson (1989) *Children's Mathematical Frameworks 8–13: A Study of Classroom Teaching*. Windsor: NFER-Nelson.

Hart, S. (1998) 'A sorry tail: ability, pedagogy and educational reform', *British Journal of Educational Studies* 46(2): 153–168.

Haslam, S. A., J. Salvatore, T. Kessler and D. Reiche (2008) 'How Stereotyping Yourself Contributes to Your Success (or Failure)', *Scientific American Mind* 23 (April).

Heifetz, R. A., M. Linsky and A. Grashow (2009) *The Practice of Adaptive Leadership: Tools and Tactics for Changing Your Organization and the World*. Boston, MA: Harvard University Press.

Holzman, L. (2000) 'Performative psychology: An untapped resource for educators', *Education and Child Psychology* 17(3): 86–101.

Holzman, L. (2009) *Vygotsky at Work and Play*. New York and Hove: Routledge.

Howe, C. and N. Mercer (2007) 'Children's social development, peer interaction and classroom learning', *Primary Review Research Survey 2/1b*, Cambridge: University of Cambridge, Faculty of Education.

Keenan, P. A. and P. J. Carnevale (1989) 'Positive effects of within-group cooperation on between-group negotiation', *Journal of Applied Social Psychology* 19: 977–992.

Kutnick, P., J. Sebba, P. Blatchford *et al.* (2002) 'Pupil Groupings in Primary School Classrooms: sites for learning and social pedagogy?' *British Educational Research Journal* 2(1): 187–206.

Kutnick, P., J. Sebba, P. Blatchford *et al.* (2005) *An Extended Review of Pupil Grouping in Schools*. London: DfES.

Lakoff, G. and M. Johnson (1980) *Metaphors We Live By*. Chicago: University of Chicago Press.

Lamon, S. (2005) *Teaching Fractions and Ratios for Understanding. Essential Content Knowledge and Instructional Strategies for Teachers (second edition)*. New York and London: Routledge.

Langer, E. J. (1989) *Mindfulness*. Cambridge MA: Da Capo Press.

Langer, E. J. (1997) *The Power of Mindful Learning*. Cambridge MA: Da Capo Press.

Lave, J. (1988) *Cognition in Practice: Mind, Mathematics and Culture in Everyday Life*. Cambridge: Cambridge University Press.

Lave, J. and E. Wenger (1991) *Situated Learning: Legitimate Peripheral Participation*. Cambridge: Cambridge University Press.

Lerch, F. J., C. Gonzalez and C. Lebiere (1999) 'Learning under high cognitive workload'. *Proceedings of the Twenty-first Conference of the Cognitive Science Society*. Mahwah, NJ, Lawrence Erlbaum Associates.

Leung, F. K. S. (2002) 'Behind the High Achievement of East Asian Students', *Educational Research and Evaluation* 8(1): 87–108.

Lo, M. L., W. Y. Pong and P. P. M. Chik (eds) (2005) *For Each and Everyone: Catering for Individual Differences Through Learning Studies*. Hong Kong: Hong Kong University Press.

Madson, P. R. (2005) *Improv Wisdom: Don't Prepare, Just Show Up*. New York: Bell Tower.

Marativa, A. and A. Iriki (2004) 'Tools for the body (schema)', *Trends in Cognitive Science* 8(2): 79–86.

Marton, F. and S. Booth (1997) *Learning and Awareness*. Mahwah, NJ: Lawrence Erlbaum Associates.

Marton, F., U. Runesson and A. B. M. Tsui (2004) 'The space of learning', in F. Marton with A. B. M. Tsui, P. P. M. Cjik *et al. Classroom Discourse and the Space of Learning*. Mahwah, NJ: Lawrence Erlbaum Associates.

Marton, F., A. B. M. Tsui, P. P. N. Cjik *et al.* (2004) *Classroom Discourse and the Space of Learning*. Mahwah, NJ: Lawrence Erlbaum Associates.

Marton, F., D. Watkins and C. Tangs (1997) 'Discontinuities and continuities in the experience of learning: an interview study of high-school students in Hong Kong', *Learning and Instruction* 7(1): 21–48.

Mathieu, W. A. (1991) *The Listening Book: Discovering Your Own Music*. Boston and London: Shambala.

Mercer, N. (1995) *The Guided Construction of Knowledge: Talk amongst teachers and learners*. Clevedon, UK: Multilingual Matters.

Mercer, N. (2000) *Words and Minds: How we use language to think together*. London: Routledge.

Millett, A., M. Askew and M. Brown (2004) 'The Impact of the National Numeracy Strategy in Year 4: (II) Teaching', in O. McNamara, *Research in Mathematics Education* 6(1): 191–205.

National Institute on Student Achievement, Curriculum and Assessment (1998) *The Educational System in Japan: Case Study Findings*, Washington DC: US Department of Education.

National Research Council (2001) *Adding it up: Helping Children Learn Mathematics*. Washington DC: National Academy Press.

Neville, B. (2005) *Educating Psyche: Emotion, Imagination and the Unconscious in Learning (second edition)*. Melbourne: Flat Chat Press.

Noddings, N. (2002) *Educating Moral People: A Caring Alternative to Character Education*. New York and London: Teachers College Press.

Noddings, N. (2005) *The Challenge to Care in Schools: An Alternative Approach to Education (second edition)*. New York and London: Teachers College Press.

Nottingham, J. (2010) *Challenging Learning*. Berwick upon Tweed: JN Publishing.

Nunes, T., D. W. Carraher and A. D. Schliemann (1993) *Street Mathematics and School Mathematics (Learning in Doing: Social, Cognitive & Computational Perspectives)*. Cambridge: Cambridge University Press.

Ofsted (2008) *Mathematics: Understanding the score*. London: HMSO.

Olive, J. and L. P. Steffe (2002) 'The construction of an iterative fractional scheme: the case of Joe', *The Journal of Mathematical Behaviour* 20(4): 413–437.

Robitaille, D. and M. Dirks (1982) 'Models for the mathematics curriculum', *For the Learning of Mathematics* 2(3): 3–21.

Rubin, R. and J. Weisberg (2003) *In an Uncertain World*. New York: Random House.

Runesson, U. (2005) 'Beyond discourse and interaction. Variation: a critical aspect for teaching and learning mathematics', *Cambridge Journal of Education* 35(1): 69–87.

Russell, B. (2000) *The Autobiography of Bertrand Russell*. New York and London: Routledge.

Sawyer, K. (2007) *Group Genius: the Creative Power of Collaboration*. New York: Basic Books.

Sawyer, R. K. (1999) 'The emergence of creativity', *Philosophical Psychology* 12(4): 447–469.

Senge, P. (2006) *The Fifth Discipline: The Art and Practice of the Learning Organization (second edition)*. New York and London: Random House.

Sergiovanni, T. J. (1999) *Building Community in Schools*. San Francisco: Jossey-Bass.

Shenk, D. (2010) *The Genius in All of Us: Why Everything You've Been Told About Genes, Talent and Intelligence is Wrong: The New Science of Genes, Talent and Human Potential*. London: Icon Books.

Siegler, R. S. and G. B. Ramani (2009) 'Playing linear number board games – but not circular ones – improves low-income preschoolers' numerical understanding', *Journal of Educational Psychology* 101(3): 545–560.

Simon, M. A. (2006) 'Key developmental understandings in mathematics: a direction for investigating and establishing learning goals', *Mathematical Thinking and Learning* 8(4): 359–371.

Simon, M. A., R. Tzur, K. Heinz, M. Kinzai and M. S. Smith (2000) 'Characterizing a perspective underlying the practice of mathematics teachers in transition', *Journal for Research in Mathematics Education* 31(5): 579–601.

Sinclair, J. and M. Coulthard (1975) *Towards an Analysis of Discourse*. Oxford: Oxford University Press.

Steffe, L. P. (2002) 'A new hypothesis concerning children's fractional knowledge', *The Journal of Mathematical Behaviour* 20(3): 267–307.

Stickgold, R. and J. M. Ellenbogen (2008) 'Sleep on It: How Snoozing Makes You Smarter', *Scientific American Mind* (August).

Stigler, J. W. and J. Hiebert (1999) *The Teaching Gap: Best Ideas From the World's Teachers for Improving Education in the Classroom*. New York: Free Press.

Tobin, K. (1986) 'Effects of teacher wait time on discourse characteristics in mathematics and language arts classes', *American Educational Research Journal* 23(2): 191–200.

Vygotsky, L. S. (1978) *Mind in Society*. Cambridge, MA: Harvard University Press.

Vygotsky, L. S. (1986) *Thought and Language*. Cambridge, MA: MIT Press.

Walkerdine, V. (1984) 'Developmental psychology and the child-centred pedagogy' in J. Henriques, W. Holloway, C. Unwin, C. Venn and V. Walkerdine, *Changing the Subject*. London: Methuen.

Walkerdine, V. (1988) *The Mastery of Reason: Cognitive Development and the Production of Rationality*. London: Routledge.

Watson, A. and J. Mason (2005) *Mathematics as a Constructive Activity: Learners Generating Examples (Studies in Mathematical Thinking & Learning)*. New York and London: Routledge.

Wood, D. J., J. S. Bruner and G. Ross (1976) 'The role of tutoring in problem solving', *Journal of Child Psychology and Psychiatry* 17: 89–100.

Young-Loveridge, J. M., M. Carr and B. Peters (1995) *Enhancing the Mathematics of Four-Year-Olds: The EMI-4s study*. Hamilton, NZ: University of Waikato.

Young-Loveridge, J., M. Taylor, S. Sharma and N. Ngarewa (2006) 'Students' perspectives on the nature of mathematics' in *Identities, cultures and learning spaces* (Proceedings of the 29th Annual Conference of the Mathematics Education Research Group of Australasia), Sydney: MERGA.

Index